Art: A Complete and Utter History

(without the boring bits)

John Farman is British and lives in South West London. He has an MA (Design) from the Royal College of Art. He has worked extensively in advertising and publishing but up until the time of writing this book didn't know his art from his elbow.

Other books by John Farman

THE VERY BLOODY HISTORY OF BRITAIN
(without the boring bits)

A SUSPICIOUSLY SIMPLE HISTORY OF SCIENCE AND INVENTION
(without the boring bits)

KEEP OUT OF THE REACH OF PARENTS

YOU CAN'T TELL A ROOK BY ITS COVER

ART A Complete and Utter History

(WITHOUT THE BORING BITS)

JOHN FARMAN

who also drew (some of) the pictures

MACMILLAN

First published 1994 by Macmillan Children's Books

This edition published 1995 by Macmillan Children's Books
a division of Macmillan Publishers Ltd

Cavaye Place London SW10 9PG
and Basingstoke

Associated companies throughout the world

ISBN 0 330 33046 2

1 3 5 7 9 8 6 4 2

A CIP catalogue record for this book is available from the British Library

Phototypeset by Intype, London

Printed and bound in Great Britain by
Mackays of Chatham PLC, Chatham, Kent

Contents

Introduction

Writing about art is like dancing about architecture.

Anon

I recently read a quote by the great American cartoon stripper Robert Crumb (Fritz the Cat's creator) which caused me to giggle at its audacity and start on the long road to finding out whether I agreed with him or not. He said, ' "ART" is just a racket! A hoax on the public by so-called "artists" who set themselves up on a pedestal and are promoted by sissy ivory-tower intellectuals and sob-sister "critics" who think the world owes them a living.'

How many times has that thought crossed my mind and how many times have I simply not had the confidence in my powers of argument (or any background knowledge) to even suggest it. Have you ever inadvertently flicked to BBC2, to witness some boring, bow-tied, big-trousered art historian spouting about a seemingly straightforward representation in paint of a seemingly straightforward subject? Did you wonder whether he's talking about the same thing as you're looking at?

Faced with a canvas that bears a strong relationship to an untuned television test card, with a price tag that would feed India for a couple of years, or when guys like Richard Long pile up some old rocks in some Godforsaken wasteland, call it something unintelligible and then pile up more loot than the price of a good two-up, two-down in Croydon, you must have questioned whether someone, somewhere is taking the pi-Pissarro?

The joke is, we all know the price of apples; how much our house is worth (or was), which of the three half-wits on *Blind Date* would be marginally less tiresome than the others, etc. etc., but when it comes to art we nervously look round, shuffle uncomfortably, and hope that the person next to us is going to venture an opinion first. I heard that on a TV programme recently some joker hung a Picasso worth millions on the Hyde Park railings, priced the same as all the other stuff, and next to a framed Xerox of his own bum. Guess which one sold? It's madness! I'm pretty jolly sure if I went to a car auction full of dreary Escorts or Cavaliers, I wouldn't be fooled if some clever-dick had slipped his Ferrari in for a laugh.

The point is that your average non-artist is as reluctant to voice his opinions about art as the Archbishop of Canterbury about break-dancing (sorry! bad example – he would). It's weird. We can be almost proud about knowing nothing about things like sport, farming, or car mechanics, but are made to feel stupid if we don't know our art from our elbow.

So, if you're one of those people that thinks that Caravaggio is an Italian motor home, or Botticelli a kind of pasta, then fear not. You too can be an expert like what I am. By the time you've read this mighty work, not only will you be able to recite all the great art movements through history but also who the big figures were, what they did and, with a bit of luck, who they did it to. The next time the after-dinner chat breaks from whether AIDS or John Major will kill us all first, try slipping in something like: 'Do you think that the Italian Futurist movement was directly, or indirectly, responsible for the rise of Fascism in Mussolini's Italy?' If your luck runs like mine, however, you'll probably have some clever-dick like Melvyn Bragg next to you – who'll probably know. Still, serves you right for mixing with such company.

CHAPTER I

Painting Before Paint

Cave Art

I couldn't tell you precisely who it was that first decided to try his (or her) hand at painting images of the things around him (or her), but historians tell us that it was probably someone not long (give or take a few million years) out of monkeydom who was no doubt fed up with looking at the bare walls of his (or her) cave.

Art equipment suppliers were a bit thin on the ground thirty thousand years ago so young *Homo erectus* had to not only invent his own 'paint' but also something to slap it on the walls with. The pigments he used were almost certainly iron or manganese oxides, giving him yellow, red and black and it seems he mixed them with animal fats or urine. Later on, up Egypt way, early painters filled out their palette by using natural ochres (browns and yellows), ground malachite (greens), and lapis lazuli (blue).

Brushes as such had still to be thought of so he had to either use his hands, bits of fur, chewed sticks or blow pipes. Having just described how early paint was made, however, the idea of filling one's mouth and blowing the filthy mixture across your living room doesn't really appeal. The modern aerosol might carve dirty great holes in the ozone layer, but it's much better for oral hygiene.

The South of France, with its warm climate and pretty girls, has always attracted artists, so it's no surprise that the oldest paintings were found in caves at Lascaux. Having said that, there were no blonde bimbos in the early paintings as, firstly, they hadn't turned up yet and, secondly, these early painters only just got the hang of animals, but were lousy at people. In fact, they usually resorted to stick people, with men and women being told apart by the employment of an extra stick (if you get my drift).

The daft-looking animals that appear on their walls often have arrows and spears sticking out of them. Many experts say this was a sort of magic to bring the hairy hunters luck – a bit like sticking pins in a figure of someone you don't like – and that the decorated caves were shrines and temples. I personally think it was probably a macho way of showing off to their wives and nippers just how clever and brave they'd been, like a framed snap over the mantelpiece of Uncle Ernie holding a prize fish.

Another somewhat dubious argument goes along the lines that primitive artists were just as capable of producing accurate likenesses as we are today, and that the bizarre animals and people were just impressions, in much the same way as Tom and Jerry are cartoon versions of a cat and a mouse. This seems about as likely as me saying that the reason I'm not a top class athlete is that I don't want to make other people seem inferior.

Obviously we'll never know the answers to these riddles. All we can safely say is that these early daubings, along with strange carvings in bone and rock, must be the beginnings of the history of art and the first of loads of interminable and unsettlable arguments.

Great Cave-Painting Names to Drop

Bit of a problem here. People in those days probably only grunted at each other, and certainly hadn't the wherewithal to actually sign anything.

CHAPTER 2

Phabulous Pharaoh-land

Egypt from 3000BC

If most of our arty ideas came from the Greeks, who did they get their ideas from? Answer – the Egyptians.

Art hadn't progressed much beyond the efforts of our old friend Erectus, apart from the work of various Indians and primitive races. It's fair to say, therefore, that the first continuous efforts in art carried the 'made in Egypt' label. Everyone knows about the pyramids, and that the kings, or pharaohs, were so rich and powerful that with a little persuasion (whips and spears) they could get thousands of their long-suffering slaves to sweat their guts out on their behalf. You must have seen pictures of the poor devils digging up the rocks, pulling them for miles overland and piling them up in pointed heaps just so that the boss could have somewhere nice to lie with his goodies when dead.

The paintings and drawings that covered the walls of these tombs are fascinating because they show a completely new way of representing man and his surroundings. It's crazy, when you realize that they were locked away purely for the pleasure of the dead pharaoh's soul and to be seen by nobody else. I bet old Tutankhamun would turn in his tomb if he knew that anyone these days can buy a reproduction of his personal (if dead) face on a cheap postcard or the front of a T-shirt saying 'I Love King Tut'.

But what was so special about the way the Egyptians represented the world about them? For a start, the artist in those days was only bothered with essentials and reproduced everything in terms of almost geometric regularity. They wouldn't have prettiness in the pyramid, so there was no fussy decoration mucking up the walls; the Egyptians were far more interested in recording everything that had been going on in the clearest way possible.

Anonymous Egyptian artist *c.*50 BC

They therefore didn't fiddle around with perspective (on account of they didn't know how it worked), tending to reduce all around them, including people, to pictures resembling plans or maps. If a duck, for instance, was shown swimming in a pond, the pond would be shown from above, but the poor duck would be lying on its side.

If you can imagine a giant steam-roller flattening everything in sight, the artist's job would be to follow (metaphorically speaking), scraping up each object and placing it in his landscape, rather like a little kid does. Look at the way a child puts the blue band across the top of the paper to represent the sky and the green at the bottom for the land. If they believe the world's flat, then why not show it that way. It's pure Egyptian logic.

The size of men, women and children was dictated by their actual importance rather than their physical dimensions or distance from the viewer. I don't think the feminist movement got much of a look-in up ancient Egypt way, as women often came out about half the size of men. Egyptian artists always drew both hands and both feet the same on either sex. Hence the expression – two left feet.

Bearing all this in mind, however, everything was drawn extremely realistically (albeit flattened) so that, even today, species of birds and animals can be easily recognized (especially if they've just been flattened).

Every Egyptian artist/craftsman had to follow this prescribed style. There was no interest in individual interpretation and the status of the artist was, unlike today, dictated by how conventional and traditional he could be. No room for Abstract Expressionism there. Artists (maybe rightly) were no more important than anyone else and certainly didn't go in for the striped sweater and beret, or any other instantly identifying eccentricity for that matter!

The result of all this was that no one took any chances, so these early artworks differed little from those produced over a thousand years later, which makes life a lot easier for the art critic (though why anyone should want to make *their* lives easier I can't imagine).

Sumerians

Although the Egyptian empire was the most powerful and influential around at that time, there were others. The Sumerians lived in Mesopotamia (the valley of the Euphrates and Tigris rivers) before the Assyrians and Akkadians. They were also important artists, although little remains of their work, owing to their annoying habit of working on sun-baked clay, which just fell to bits, unlike the stone used by the Egyptians.

Another reason for the scarcity of artefacts around these days was that, unlike the Egyptians, who believed that the human body and its likeness must be preserved if the soul is to continue, the Sumerians buried their kings with their whole household, slaves and all – so that they wouldn't get too lonely in the next life. As jobs went, slaving certainly left a lot to be desired.

So instead of lavishly decorated tombs, people in those days preferred huge gruesome monuments to their great victories. You can imagine the sort of thing – kings trampling the crushed bodies of the vanquished who screamed in vain for mercy. Certainly not the stuff to hang in your average front room.

They weren't that bright, however, those old Mesopotamians. They reckoned that if they kept all those pictures on the wall of their foes being well and truly thrashed by their brave soldier lads, it would prevent them ever being conquered again. Nice thinking, but an idea that could severely backfire.

Later on in Assyrian times these pictures turned out like comic strips, telling the whole bloody story of the king's victories, and became a great clue for us nosy past-watchers as to how they lived (and fought). Rather like war-reporting these days (where military leaders always make out that, although they've wiped out trillions of the enemy, casualties on the home side are relatively light), the Assyrians went one better. In their carved monuments they show mounds of the dead foe, but none of their own. If you were to believe these images you might be tempted to think that wars were pretty fab in those days (providing you were on the right side).

Great Egyptian or Sumerian Artists' Names to Drop

As you might have gathered, still no names. Trying to find the name of an Egyptian artist is about as easy as finding the name of an Egyptian baker.

CHAPTER 3

Time to Start Proper Art

Greece in the Seventh Century BC

I suppose if one mentions Greece these days one is hard put to think of anything much outside hot holidays and rather indifferent hosts. Difficult to believe that this is the country whose people invented sport, revolutionized the arts and were first to stuff the vine leaf.

It all began in the seventh century BC in Crete, the largest Greek island. At that time kings were two a penny, and the Cretin – sorry, Cretan – ones were by far the richest, having made all their cash from trading. Well, that's if you call taking loads of valuable goods off trusting foreigners but forgetting to pass over any cash, trading!

Being on an island, Cretan artists were much more fortunate than their poor relatives on the mainland who, every time they got their brushes or chisels out, had some horrible European horde or other trampling over what they were hoping to paint or carve. Not only that, but these ruffians came from a place where no one could draw for toffee and even when they tried, the toffees still looked decidedly two dimensional – positively Egyptian.

Nikothenes *Boxers* 500–525 BC

Gradually the artists on the mainland, through peering enviously across the water at what the Cretans were doing, got the hang of art and started producing some of their own. Instantly noticeable were the buildings, which became very huge and very plain: this was the Doric style. The Dorics were a rather grumpy tribe to which the Spartans, who actually gave their name to not having a good time, belonged. At least these Greek buildings were built for living, breathing people, however, unlike the Egyptians who only seemed to build their huge pointed constructions for rich stiffs, while the peasants had to grovel around in horrid sandy tents.

Again, unlike the Egyptians, who'd simply refused to actually look at what they were sculpting or drawing, the Greeks almost discovered the human body, surprising when you think that almost everyone must have had one (even the Egyptians). This was fine as far as their sculpture went, but when it came to drawing, they still had a hard time. The few remaining pieces from that period show only half-hearted attempts at breaking away from that old, flat, sideways-on style of the Egyptians.

The Great Breakthrough

One of the greatest dates in Western art came around 500BC – a breakthrough that almost went unnoticed but was to open the door for art to develop and flourish unhindered. It was almost like hearing about the invention of a new primary colour, and it heralded the great revolution in art and, in terms of across-the-board culture, even human history.

A run-of-the-mill, high-street jug painter broke all the rules and, would you believe it . . . drew a foot from the front! All that and we don't even know the poor devil's name. His timing was perfect as science and philosophy were stirring from a deep slumber, all the farfetched myths and legends about those two-a-penny gods (Zeus, Aphrodite etc.) began to be questioned, and theatre, in the form we now recognize, was born. Artists became obsessed with the human form and how to represent it in either two or three dimensions. OK, they were still regarded as a subspecies by the rather sissy intellectuals and noblemen, but it was a picnic compared to the rotten treatment that had been dished out to the Egyptian artists, who were treated no better than slaves by those fearful pharaohs.

PERICLES

Around 450BC Pericles, who'd just put paid to the Persians, began to rebuild what they'd knocked down in Athens, but this time in really flash materials like marble and bronze and to a degree of magnificence never seen before. Not only that, but the gossip columnists of the day relate that he treated artists as his equals (shock horror!), particularly a guy called Phidias whom he put in charge of sculpting all the gods and generally sprucing up the interiors of the new flash temples.

Unfortunately little remains of what was produced in Athens during that period, unless you count all the copies of the statues the Romans produced for the tourists, or for their own loos and back gardens. Indeed it's often only through the touristy knick-knacks (not donkeys in sombreros!) brought back from early Greek hols, that we have any idea of what those fantastic Athenian artists had been up to.

Watch Out, There's Christians About

Those narrow-minded old Christians, who, typical of most fanatical religious followers, thought their God (Jesus's dad) was the only one worth worshipping, destroyed anything remotely non-Christian, wiping out some of the finest art ever.

One of these pieces, by Pericles' aforementioned mate Phidias, was a thirty-six-foot wooden lady called Pallas Athene and covered in gold, ivory, semi-precious stones and just about everything valuable he could lay his hands on. She must have scared the temple-goers stiff as she stood, so legend remembers, in the doorway of the Parthenon in a hat with a gold griffon on it and with her huge pet snake peeking rather unpleasantly from behind her shield. Unfortunately the original was lost in some war or other so we again only have a rather inferior Roman copy to go on.

The Greeks were really the first to try to find out how the human body worked and strove like demons to show off this new knowledge, even hidden under drapery. It was this skill that made them revered and continually returned to for inspiration by artists intent on working out how to draw and sculpt their fellow man (and woman).

There's little doubt that Greek artists were encouraged by the constant demand for sculptures and images of the great sportspersons of the time as decoration for temples. Weird really! I can't imagine huge statues of Fatima Whitbread or even the weeping Gazza inside St Paul's Cathedral, especially when you consider that Greek athletes never wore a stitch. Unfortunately, just like before, little remains of these statues owing to an annoying habit of the common Middle Ages folk of melting them down for the bronze simply to make pots and pans. One of the only unharmed figures found at Delphi was of an anonymous charioteer who looked like a slightly happier John McEnroe (if you can imagine that). Despite this unhappy connection, there is a simplicity and even beauty about this figure that surpasses any copy.

The World Wakes Up

Art went into turbo charge in the hundred years between 520 and 420BC. By the end of the fifth century *hoi polloi* had begun to really appreciate what wonderful stuff was being done and, more to the point, the artists themselves were well aware that they were breaking totally new ground. People in the street would discuss the merits of the various schools which, in turn, promoted a kind of competitiveness that made those artist chappies work even harder. Yet again, little evidence of this frenzy of creation remains apart from a few old pots and vases, and we can only get a faint idea of their subtlety by later imitations. One criticism of their sculpture would be that every figure seems to have had the same head. We accept that the Greeks might have been a good-looking race (whatever happened?), but surely they couldn't all have had perfect features. There was obviously no attempt at individual likenesses either because they just couldn't do it or, more likely, they were desperate to suck up to the guy who was paying the drachmas. It was only towards the end of the fourth century that artists started sneaking in the odd furrow in the brow, wrinkle round the eye or hint of a smile.

The statue of Alexander the Great taken from an earlier portrait by Lysippus (no surnames in those days), although a little short in the nose department at least makes the great hero look like a real living, breathing man as opposed to a sort of Greek Chippendale. Whether Alexander looked like that or not we'll never know, but we do know he was to have a great influence on Greek art.

Trojan *c.*AD 100

His habit of conquering countries obviously gave the artists a much wider audience.

No longer is the art of that period called Greek; now it was to have a new title – Hellenistic, following the collective name given to all the empires founded by Alex and his successors. The gentle, almost lyrical, classical stuff gave way to a far more rumbustious, violent style, which is not surprising when one considers that all those Greeks ever seemed to do in those days was fight each other.

Laocoon *Agusander, Athendoros and Polydoros of Rome* Second century BC

Typical of the art of this period was a sculpture uncovered in Rome from the workshop of Hagesandrus, Athenodorus and Polydorus of Rhodes. It depicts what happened to a poor guy called Laocoon and his sons. Apparently Laocoon, a Trojan priest, had tipped off his mates about accepting this huge wooden horse which had turned up outside the gates and was being offered as a goodwill gesture by the Greeks who'd been trying to get in. Laocoon reckoned (quite rightly) that this naff pressie could well have a bellyful of extremely indigestible Greek soldiers who, once inside the gates, would rape and pillage the good folk of Troy willy-nilly.

But it seems that the Greek gods, who were behind this nifty trick, were well pissed off with Laocoon for attempting to muck up their plans, so they sent a couple of huge snakes to give the poor priest and his two sons a none-too-friendly squeeze.

Sculptures of this ilk appealed greatly to a population whose idea of a good time on a Saturday afternoon was to take the family down the local colosseum and watch gladiators making kebabs of each other, or watch their pet lions sampling tasty Christians. It is said that when this incredible piece was discovered in Rome, over one and a half thousand years later, a certain young man called Michelangelo, who just happened to be passing, was knocked out by it.

Art for the Home

By the end of the second century BC most Greek sculpture was made on commission to Rome, which was the up and coming centre of art and the main fan of Greek culture. The artists themselves began to attract great attention as individuals, and it became a status symbol to use the most famous to decorate your villa. All this would have been lost had it not been for the eruption of Vesuvius whose lava, though hot and horrid, managed to preserve a lot of the domestic art (and kill off most of the population of Pompeii). Ah well, it's an ill volcano that blows no one any good.

You've only got to see some of the stuff painted purely as decoration for a rich Pompeian's bathroom to see just how far they had progressed in the representation of three-dimensional figures and landscapes on a flat surface! Admittedly they didn't yet know the rules of perspective, but they had a pretty good stab at it all the same.

First to Fourth Centuries AD

When the Romans conquered the rest of the known world, Rome naturally became the centre of all things artistic, and imitating the Greeks was still all the rage (as they were by far the best at it). The new architecture was awe inspiring, the most fab (and big) building being the Colosseum, which used not one, or two, but three different Greek styles. Their extravagant use of arches was employed all over their empire from Italy and France to North Africa and Asia. Wherever there was a valley that needed something to span it, the Romans would throw up an arched aqueduct or bridge.

They also pinched the Greeks' painting methods as well. Unlike the rich Greeks, Roman patrons were quite happy to have accurate, non-flattering portraits. These can now be checked against the death masks that were also all the rage. We therefore, for the first time in history, know what all-time greats like Pompey, Augustus, Titus or Nero really looked like, as if they'd just been in the papers. Artists also copied the Greeks' ability to portray great battles in stone and paint so that they could show all the ordinary Romans at home how brave their leaders were (and where all the money was going).

After Christ was born it only took a couple of hundred years or so before Hellenistic and Roman art smothered the culture of their vanquished oriental kingdoms. The Egyptians, for instance, still buried their mothers as mummies, and fathers as mummies, but started copying Greek-style painting to decorate the tombs. Some of the craftsmen, once they'd got the hang of it, produced staggering work that sometimes even surpassed what they'd been trying to copy. In the painting of a dead Egyptian we can see a painting that could almost have been done in the twentieth century by one of the Post Impressionists.

Christianity Creeps Up

When Christianity started creeping across from the East the traditions of Greek art were still called upon to help in the representation of the Saviour and his lads, even though the poor Greeks were now regarded as pagans (gratitude or what?). There was, however, a slight problem as the Christian religion forbade the creation of graven images – a bit of a hitch if you were in the graven image business, so they compromised by only doing things that showed what a good sort God was.

There then followed a period when, throughout the shrinking Roman Empire, a sort of weird crossover art existed, as the Greeks' wonderful realism gave way to the same kind of naïve symbolism that they'd originally replaced. Sculptors couldn't be bothered to blunt their chisels on marble, so used a much softer stone and crude drills to hack out the odd ear or eye.

There could be a thousand reasons why painters forgot how to paint and draw like the Greeks. Many historians believe they got bored with all that realistic stuff and wanted to attempt a sort of impressionism. I'm inclined to believe they just became lazy and, after a while, simply forgot how to do it.

Great Greek Artists' Names to Drop

Euthymides, Myron, Praxiteles, Lysippus.

CHAPTER 4

Learning to Forget

Rome and Byzantium, Fifth to Thirteenth Centuries AD

When Christianity became the Empire's top religion in AD311, thanks to Emperor Constantine, everything changed. Instead of the Christians meeting in poky little church halls, they now had the clout to build big. They didn't want enormous temples like those of the 'pagan' Greeks; instead they built vast church halls like the old 'basilicas' (royal halls).

Next problem was how to decorate them. They couldn't have statues of God, saints or miscellaneous angels ('graven images'), and anyway the poor new converts wouldn't be able to see the difference between them and their dear old defunct ones; come to that, how do you make a statue of a god who's supposed to be invisible? Exactly!

They weren't that keen on paintings either until Pope Gregory the Great pointed out, at the end of the sixth century AD, that most of the people who now went in their church couldn't read or write. This meant they could only work out what the priests were going on about by looking at the pictures.

Nice one, Greg. If you hadn't said that when you did, the whole history of art could have stopped there, and so could I. Just think, this might have been the last page. Phew! Having said that, painting was only allowed for the furtherance of God and, quality-wise, declined rapidly. God might have had the best tunes, but he didn't have the best art and the more simple and symbolic it became, the more the wonderful knowledge of the Greeks slipped through their 'holey' fingers. Eventually it all came to resemble a kind of slightly Greek-flavoured, primitive art.

Not everyone went along with the liberalism of Pope Gregory, however, and in the eastern part of the Roman Empire, its capital,

Byzantium (later Constantinople, and much later Istanbul), was taken over by a group in AD745 that banned religious painting altogether. When this decree gradually relented, the paintings that emerged, though awful, had an oriental look but still showed traces of the old Greek style. This Byzantine style was to spread back throughout the Empire and can still be seen in the work of the 'icon' makers of Russia (they always were a bit behind the times).

CHAPTER 5

Meanwhile . . .

Early Eastern Art

So far we've spent our time looking at what was going on in Egypt and Greece, without a thought for what they were up to out in the Far East. One of the big problems that the Eastern artists from this time faced was that anything that looked remotely like a person was shunned by the new religions that were sweeping from the Middle East. Rather than risk being parted from their best painting hand for doing a quick sketch of their chums, they decided to stick to symbols and patterns (and would you blame them?). These became complex and extremely beautiful, like the Eastern rugs that fetch fortunes today. The symbolism very often told stories, rather like modern cartoon strips.

Even when the Persians and Indians did get round to easing a few odd people into their pictures (around the fourteenth century) they didn't begin to attempt to make them look realistic, tending to follow the Egyptian 'flat, side on, look'. In fact the paintings looked a bit like animated rugs.

The Chinese

The Chinese, on the other hand, who had always kept themselves to themselves, had gone streets ahead. After all, if you work in a vacuum, you are either going to break new ground, or stay exactly the same. Instead of producing all that angular stuff like the Egyptians, the Chinese tended to make their images from circles and swirling curves, which lent themselves much more to realism and movement. It took the rest of the world ages to catch up with their knowledge of drawing, perspective and anatomy.

The other major difference was that, unlike the rest of the world, the Chinese rated their creative people higher than the butcher, baker and noodle maker. They weren't exactly chased down the street for their autographs, but at least they were shown a respect hitherto unseen elsewhere.

Mind you, artists in China weren't known for having a lot of free time, as drawings weren't something they could toss off when they had a spare minute. Owing to their belief in deep meditation, they were required to sit and contemplate for hours, and sometimes days, before putting pen or brush to parchment. In fact, it was nothing in those days for monks and artists (actually, most of the artists were monks, and monks, artists) to sit for ages simply contemplating a leaf, a rock or a puddle. Having said all that, I suppose if you're making a decent living, it can't be all bad.

Pictures weren't hung over the mantelpiece in ancient China, but rather kept in scrolls in the sideboard, to be brought out reverently and pored over and studied for hours on end, a bit like we might do with books.

The other thing they weren't wild about was trolling out into the chilly Chinese countryside with their sketch scrolls under their arms. Oh no, they preferred to sit and study a scene for goodness knows how long before returning to the comfort of their homes to draw what they remembered; but their memory wasn't always very good. What tended to happen was that they usually drew all their landscapes in the same (idealized) way – rather like the stuff you see on the walls of Chinese takeaways. You know, a ridiculously high mountain, with a load of mist swirling round a few flattish fir trees at the base, and halfway up, in tiny detail, a couple of strangely dressed Chinese persons struggling up (or down).

All velly well, but I bet if your average man in the Chinese street was looking through his scrolls, of an evening, to find somewhere nice to take the kids on holiday, he'd have been a bit hard put to find anywhere remotely different.

The Chinese did, however, become absolute masters of the brush. They worked in the same water-soluble inks that you can still buy in delicate little blocks today, and used the same variety of fine brushes. To see a top Chinese artist painting a goldfish, for instance, with just a few strokes, leaves your average European watercolour painter breathless.

Eastern art hardly changed while the quality and style throughout the rest of the world was to ebb and flow like the ocean. The great Japanese master, Hokusai, for instance, produced paintings in the eighteenth and nineteenth centuries that simply looked like more modern versions of the stuff his ancestors had been doing thousands of years before.

Great Chinese Artists' Names to Drop

Try Ku K'ai-Chi, Ma Yüan, Kao K'o Kung, Liu Ts'ai or Hidenobu. Let's face it, I bet I could have written anything and you'd be none the wiser.

CHAPTER 6

Painting in the Dark

Europe in the Sixth to Eleventh Centuries AD

After the collapse of the Holy Roman Empire, there followed a period in history that has come to be known as the Dark Ages:

1) because the world was thrown into darkness as far as progress was concerned and . . .
2) because it went on for ages (five hundred years to be precise).

In fact we know very little about the art of the period that preceded the Europe we more or less know today. It seems incredible to us these days that everything seemed to stand still, and even fall over backwards, for five centuries.

The religious painters in particular almost took a delight in forgetting everything the Greeks had taught the world, and seemed to slip back to the flat, angular (and darn sight easier) style of the Egyptians. Unlike the Chinese, if they didn't have what they

were trying to draw practically nailed to their drawing boards, they tended to revert to the childlike images. This was obviously a little tricky if you were attempting to depict something like a battle.

Having said that, battles were often all they had to draw, for as soon as one nasty Teutonic tribe, like the Goths, disappeared out the back door, the poor peasants would have either the Vandals (who invented vandalism), Saxons, Vikings or Danes hammering at the front.

BAYEUX TAPESTRY

A good example of this bad battle-drawing came near the end of the Dark Ages and was known as the Bayeux Tapestry, sewn by the good womenfolk of Bayeux, France, which was not only the longest cartoon strip in the world but also the unfunniest. It depicted the French whipping the English (for once!) at the Battle of Hastings in 1066, and was done because, unlike these days, when one can read about stuff like Norman Conquests in the papers, hardly any of the Frogs (or anyone else for that matter) could read back in the eleventh century. They therefore had to work it out from pictures.

Bayeux Tapestry AD c.1080

The 'Dark Artists' also suffered greatly from an ancient habit of frowning at originality. After all, they thought, if you go down to the local tailor's for a suit, there's a fair chance you'll want it to look a bit like everyone else's. You don't want him to go off on his own personal flight of fancy. It was the same with art. Most church runners wanted a painting or sculpture that looked like the one they'd just seen down the road. Art was simply a commodity, and this attitude was another good reason for nothing much happening through the Dark Ages.

You might think that the only art done in the Dark Ages was done to promote religion. On the contrary, castles must have been full of fine work, but because they had a nasty habit of getting themselves knocked down almost as soon as they were built, there's precious little still around to go on. Also people tend to be a bit superstitious about chucking out the religious stuff, as the fear of a one-way trip down to the old fire and brimstone was never far from the minds of the Dark Ages peasant.

Great Dark Ages Artists' Names to Drop

Easy, there weren't any!

CHAPTER 7

God Rules OK?

Twelfth- and Thirteenth-century Art

Twelfth Century

When the light came back on after the Dark Ages in England, artists were painting more than ever in the stodgy old Egyptian style, as can be seen from the illuminated manuscripts of the time. Instead of pharaohs there were angels and instead of battles and hunting scenes there was religious symbolism. No attempt was made at realism, which is just as well as they couldn't draw to save their lives.

Mind you, this isn't always a bad thing. Very often if the artist frees himself from the need for things to look like things, it allows him (or her) much more time to cover broader concepts using other elements like design and symbolism.

I often wonder if the point at which many of us give up art is when, as children, we are forced into trying to make things look realistic (shading and stuff). Child art has the same freshness, charm and naïvety as a lot of these early paintings.

These religious painters of the twelfth century also decided to stop even bothering to mix colours from nature and used instead intense blues, reds and greens with lashings of gold for their illustrations. The best examples of this kind of work can be seen in the brilliant stained-glass windows that are still some of the finest features of our oldest churches and cathedrals in England and France (in those days we controlled half of it).

Thirteenth Century

One of the things that strikes the casual scholar of the art of this period was how much better the sculptors were becoming compared to the painters. Of course we know that the painters had long forgotten that they could get a 3D effect on a flat surface and must have watched in awe as their sculptor mates streaked ahead, creating almost lifelike copies of the people around them (not realizing the Greeks had done it much better over a thousand years before).

This wasn't helped by the way paintings were actually done. In those days it was unknown for an artist to do the whole thing from start to finish. You got someone mixing the paint, someone putting in the outline (copied from some old manuscript or other), someone filling in the colours and probably, human nature being what it is, someone taking all the flaming credit. Nobody even dreamed of picking up a sketch-parchment and trundling off into the countryside to do an honest day's drawing.

The results were often a bit haphazard, and lacked any real unity. I suppose it would be a bit like that game where someone folds a piece of paper and everyone draws a bit. When opened out, it might look funny, but it certainly ain't art.

Early Portraiture

People were drawn very much in this way. First you would take a standard body (whatever that is), then you'd maybe change his or her clothes a bit. Next, shove a standard head on the body; and then, the ultimate cop-out, write who it's supposed to be underneath.

Mind you, even the sculptors did this sort of thing. If you look at most of the old church carvings of the period, you'll notice that everyone – be it angels, apostles, Virgins, even Jesuses – has almost exactly the same face and expression (usually rather blank), give or take the odd tacked-on beard.

Great Twelfth- and Thirteenth-century Artists' Names to Drop

Sorry, folks, still no one much to write home about, except . . .

CHAPTER 8

Fame at Last

Giotto di Bondone (1266–1337)

Marco Polo was off on his holidays, our Crusaders were getting trounced by the surly Saracens and art was going nowhere. Suddenly, in the middle of all this Byzantine conservatism (bad, flat decorative drawing) came a genius from Florence, Italy, the like of whom had never been seen before. Not since the Greeks and Romans, a thousand years earlier, had anyone shown such an

Giotto *Christ's Entry into Jerusalem* 1305–6

astounding ability to handle form and colour. He alone rediscovered how to make things look solid on a flat surface. He alone managed to re-create real-life situations as if they were on stage. To the average Florentine punter, it must have been like seeing a photograph or going to the movies for the first time. Suddenly all the big religious bashes, like the Nativity, or Jesus's best tricks – walking on water, feeding of the five thousand etc. – were revealed in glorious Technicolor. Sure the sculptors had been doing it for ages, and sure Giotto must have pinched some of their ideas; but he was the first to make it work in paint, and gets the lifetime Oscar for the complete rebirth of painting in Europe.

Giotto owed some of his lasting fame to the rediscovery of *buon fresco* (true fresco), a method of painting directly on to wet lime plaster, which meant the paint didn't peel off after a few centuries. Apparently the ancient Minoans invented it when doing up their Palace of Knossos but it had been largely forgotten after the fall of the Roman Empire.

It wasn't long before our Giotto hit near rock-star fame and his Florentine fans became justly proud of him, rating him even above the ancient nameless masters. Up to that time it was almost unheard of for a painter or sculptor to sign his work (usually for good reason) and Giotto became one of the first to be identified by the work he did and, therefore, the earliest of the big name artists.

Other Giotto Firsts

1) He was the first to create an illusion of depth on a flat surface.
2) He was the first to try (in paint) to imitate real life, showing how a person would look in lots of different situations, both physical and emotional.
3) Instead of showing whole figures, and trying to cram them into his compositions, Giotto was the first to make a bit more room by placing one behind another.
4) He was the first (and maybe the last) to suggest that painting was better than sculpture.

CHAPTER 9

Art Goes International

Fourteenth-century Europe

Although for ages Giotto had been top of the painting pops in Italy, news was slow getting round the rest of Europe, let alone the world. For a first, a fab new disease called the Black Death ('cos it turned you black) was killing anything that moved and, for a second, they had only invented the mechanical clock in 1290 so nobody really knew or cared much about how long things took. These days, as you know, if you're famous you only have to blink and the world can know what you had for breakfast on the same morning.

DUCCIO DI BUONINSEGNA (1255–1319)

Throughout the rest of Europe painters were still churning out Identikit pictures: mix-and-match angels and saints with interchangeable heads. Having said that, even in Siena – which was not that far from Florence – painters like Duccio were still treading the old Byzantine path which had become increasingly dominant through the Middle Ages. OK, he'd taken it much further than anyone else, introducing a slight three-dimensional feeling, but he and two lads from his own workshop, Simone Lippi and Lippo Memmi, were still smothering everything in gold leaf and plastering the skies with fat, ugly baby angels.

On the plus side they did break from the old habit of never looking at what they were going to paint before painting it. This allowed portraiture, or at least getting a bit of individuality into the subjects, to be reborn.

At this time artists began to get out of the house a little more,

Duccio *The Annunciation c.*1308

so the Northern European painters got the chance to see how far the great Italians had broken from the pack. It became fairly commonplace for an artist to go and work in far-flung cities in far-flung countries (especially if he had the Black Death nipping at his heels). Around this time, Bohemia (a little country now in the Czech Republic) became a bit of an arty centre (hence Bohemian?), and when their Anne came over to marry our Richard II (odd, seeing as he preferred chaps), she brought with her Continental influences which delighted a Britain still floundering around trying to see the light at the end of its personal Dark Age.

The result of all this mooching around and looking over each other's shoulders resulted in something which historians now call the International Style, which can be summed up as a pure cross between the Byzantine 'flat' look and the delicately observed, lifelike and far more sensitive Italian stuff begun by Giotto. An example of the International Style is the Wilton Diptych which can be seen in London's National Gallery.

In this charming, if somewhat naïve, picture we see King Richard being presented to baby Jesus, who is obviously not that impressed as the naughty little scamp appears to be showing him a well-known two-fingered sign.

Great Fourteenth-century Artists' Names to Drop

Simone Martini (see the wonderful world of), Lippo Memmi, Pisanello, Pisano, Lorenzetti.

CHAPTER 10

The Renaissance

Early Fifteenth Century

England and France were far too busy fighting each other to worry that much about art, so it was down to the Italians to push things forward. Once again it was old Giotto who paved the way for what was called the Renaissance (rebirth). Suddenly artists became obsessed with the work of the Greeks and Romans and wanted to be at least as good as them. The fifteenth-century Italians were dying to get back a bit of the power and influence that the Romans had enjoyed over a thousand years ago before those horrid, rough Goths and Vandals mucked it all up. They had always thought that Gothic art was cr . . . ude, and as for the Vandals, we all know what they came to be remembered for.

They reckoned that a supremacy in art was one way to get back their self-respect, and so if you were a young, talented Italian and wanted to be *in* artwise, you packed your paints and hit the road for Florence which, like Paris during the back end of the nineteenth century, was where it was all at.

FILIPPO BRUNELLESCHI (1377–1446)

Leader of this aesthetic brat-pack was a young architect called Brunelleschi, who, it must be said, owed quite a bit, surprisingly, to a lot of the old Gothic construction ideas – like how to make a huge ceiling stay up (vaulting). It's interesting to note that Brunelleschi's style was copied for centuries throughout Europe and

America. Only relatively recently has there been a move away from all those often naff Italian mouldings that were plastered inside and outside otherwise rather drab buildings.

Very recently, however, there seems to be an even nastier conspiracy to build severely soppy mock-classical office blocks (much loved by Prince Charles) using what look like huge Lego pieces. The only consolation is that they appear to be so cheap and inconsequential that they'll probably be condemned before you can even say Brunelleschi.

His relevance to painting and drawing was that he gave artists a mathematical way of solving something that had been driving them round the bend for donkey's years – perspective. Even the Greeks, who'd had a fair stab at it, never really got their highly intelligent heads round how to calculate the way things appear to reduce as they get further away. Brunelleschi's arty chums must have stood him loads of drinks down the local wine bar for showing them how to do it.

Masaccio *Virgin and Child* 1426

MASACCIO (1401–28)

Of all those who became obsessed with this new skill, it was a young chap called Masaccio (nicknamed Clumsy Thomas) who staggered the Florentines when he unveiled his wall painting of the Holy Trinity in a Florentine church. His brilliant use of the newfangled perspective daubed on the back wall must have looked to them like he'd driven a JCB through it to reveal a Brunelleschi-style chapel behind. Mind you, if they were expecting a pretty International Style painting they could well have wanted their money back. Young Masaccio, who doesn't look the least bit clumsy to me, didn't like all that graceful flowing stuff with pretty flowers and jewels, so he painted a rather brutal angular tomb, with a rather sad skeleton sitting on it.

DONATELLO (1386–1466)

Top sculptor was Donato di Nicolo di Betto Bardi whose nickname was Donatello (just as well!). Although older than Masaccio he lived much longer after him – not difficult as poor Masaccio died on his twenty-eighth birthday. He had no time for what had gone before and, instead of the slightly limp, idealized, almost alien-looking Gothic statues that hung around the great cathedrals, his figures looked like real people petrified in moments of energy and concentration. This was presumably because, unlike the medieval sculptors, he actually looked at what he was carving, asking his chums to come round to his workshop to pose for him. Rather him than me. I can't imagine what my sculptures would look like if I relied on my friends.

Donatello *St George c.*1415–17

Donatello's realism often shocked the fifteenth-century viewer as he never avoided stark realism when required. When, for instance, he sculpted Herod's Feast in Siena they were able to see the horror on the guests' faces as the executioner plonked St John's head (without St John) on a plate right in front of the King. I mean, it's enough to put one off one's pasta.

JAN VAN EYCK (1390–1441)

While Donatello was knocking them dead in Italy, over in the Netherlands Jan van Eyck was having his own mini-Renaissance and raking in the big bucks from all over Northern Europe. His fame came from his almost obsessive love of detail and an ability to reproduce the delicacy of nature in a manner never seen before.

He is better known, however, for egg conservation. Let me explain. Up to that time the most normal medium used to mix the powdered colours with to make paint was egg yolk. This was used so that the artist could put down many washes of watered-down colour without ruining the underpainting (dried egg yolk is quite water resistant). Now whether Jan didn't want to waste eggs or found (more likely) that the washes tended to dry too fast we will never know. But we do know that he was one of the first to mix oil into the pigment (the actual colour), enabling him, because of its slow drying qualities, to produce immaculate gradations from one tone, or hue, to another. He had, in fact, invented oil painting. What a pity he didn't put a patent on it, as it was to become the most common medium for hundreds of years to come.

Van Eyck was not remembered for this alone, however. He was to capture a reality that almost shocked the post-medieval European art world.

His famous painting of the marriage of Arnolfini was the nearest thing to a snapshot that had ever been seen. Maybe a bit too realistic, as the young bride looks as if the wedding might be happening after the main event (nudge nudge, wink wink!). The painter had become a truthful eye-witness for the first time.

While van Eyck was busying himself with portraits, Conrad

Jan van Eyck *Giovanni Arnolfini and his Wife* 1434

Witz was doing likewise with landscapes. Up until now artists had been churning out idealized landscapes just to please their patrons. Witz, for the first time, painted on location, which meant that the place could actually be recognized.

Other Great Early Fifteenth-century Artists' Names to Drop

Ghiberti, Verrocchio, Veneziano (painter turned pizza), Conrad Witz.

CHAPTER II

Carry On Renaissance

Later Fifteenth-century Art

The English had roasted Joan of Arc but lost the Hundred Years War with France, ending up only owning Calais (le grand booby prize); Constantinople had fallen to the Turks and everyone decided to blow the final whistle and proclaim the Byzantine empire, and the Middle Ages, over.

ANDREA MANTEGNA (1431–1506)

Mantegna *St James Led to his Execution* c.1455

Back in Italy one of the staggering new painters of this era was Mantegna, who worked in Padua. He was one of the first to get to grips with the rediscovered, but still newfangled, perspective, producing pictures that provided an almost 'through the keyhole' look at everyday life in downtown Rome. Unfortunately few of his paintings remain as he had an annoying habit of painting his eggy-based pictures on dry plaster followed by an oil glaze. This method was all right for the odd couple of hundred years, but tended to fall to bits after that. If that wasn't bad enough, much of the rest of his work was blown to smithereens during the bombing of Padua during the Second World War. But Mantegna must go down in history for being one of the first artists to use perspective – not to show off, but more as a way of providing a realistic stage set to put his characters in.

PIERO DELLA FRANCESCA (1416–92)

Many would argue these days that Piero della Francesca was the greatest painter that ever lived. While Mantegna was wowing the Italians up north, Piero was doing the same in the south. His major contribution was in the use of light, which was something the medieval painters switched off: their characters, like vampires (or John Major), cast no shadows. Piero's knowledge of representing dimension and perspective (somewhat helped by being a mathematician) still leaves modern critics gobsmacked. Combined with the depth caused by his use of differing light planes (i.e. different light tones to represent different distances), it pushed him head and shoulders above his painter mates.

SANDRO BOTTICELLI (1445–1510)

Even if you haven't heard of our Sandro, there's a good chance you will have seen his most famous painting, *The Birth of Venus* (still available in all good branches of Boots). He was a Florentine painter who had a great little business churning out stacks of Madonnas and baby Jesuses for his many fans. Not for him all that complicated perspective and anatomy. No, he did very nicely, thank you, working along the old Byzantine way using bucketfuls of pink paint on fat naked ladies and their babies.

The Birth of Venus shows a rather pretty, if rather deformed, girl with a stretched neck and no shoulders standing, for some reason, in a seashell, modestly covering her rude bits from the inquisitive looks of a couple of passing angels.

Botticelli *The Birth of Venus* 1482

Botticelli fell out of favour for hundreds of years, until the Pre-Raphaelites (*see* Pre-Raphaelites p. 107) rediscovered him. They seemed to like all that sort of soppy stuff. It must be said in his defence that, as with all the other Florentine painters of the time, he saw painting as an opportunity to have fun, show off and break away from all the rather over-pious work that had gone before.

Meanwhile . . . Back in the Rest of Europe

While Italy was having a rather fab Renaissance, the rest of Europe was plodding along, trying to break out of the old Dark Ages. Architecture was still very Gothic, all pointy arches, buttresses and gargoyles, while painting was struggling under tons of gold leaf and skies teeming with halo-capped, overweight angels. In

Stephan Lochner *The Virgin and Child in the Rose Garden* 1440

The Virgin and Child in the Rose Garden, Stephan Lochner, a German artist of the by then well-dated International Style, painted a rather fed-up Virgin and an inflatable-looking child, surrounded by what looked like a load of colourful pigeons. Look closer and you'll see they're a bunch of angelings (officially seraphim and cherubim) who've got together and formed a band. Although Lochner and his mates were still more or less medieval artists, they must have had postcards from Italy, as there was definitely the beginnings of a Renaissance influence. (That is, they attempted to get a bit of depth into their pictures.)

Some of the Northern European painters saved up their pocket money and actually made it to Rome, hanging out with some of the whizz-kid Roman artists. Their influence can be seen in the work of the Frenchman Fouquet and the Netherlander Roger van der Weyden, now recognized as the missing link between the old medieval artists and the three-dimensional-looking work of Italian masters like Mantegna and Piero della Francesca.

Other Great Renaissance Names to Drop

Ghirlandaio, Perugino, and in Northern Europe Fouquet, Hugo van der Goes, Veit Stoss and Schongauer.

CHAPTER 12

High Renaissance

The 1500s

England had a brand new king – the late, great and extremely chubby Henry VIII; Spain had become the bullyboy of Europe, picking fights with, and conquering, just about everyone; and Magellan had proved the world was round by arriving back at the same place he started off from.

Italy was still extremely civilized and led the Western world culturally. If the Renaissance was good for art, then the High Renaissance art at the beginning of the Cinquecento (1500s) was even better and was to become the icing on the top of the Italian cake. Three names were to emerge that were to be top of the pops for the rest of time. Leonardo da Vinci, Michelangelo and, perhaps a little less famous, Raphael.

Having said that, they all reached almost movie star status in their own lifetime and were the first artists to call the shots and paint what, and for whom, they wanted. No longer did they have bossy Popes faxing them every five minutes ordering them to come round to paint yet another Madonna and, what should have been by then, her positively geriatric kid.

Not only did they have this new freedom, but also, much like famous singing stars turning to acting, dabbled around with other disciplines like writing, architecture, mathematics, science and the mystic secrets of the universe – and that was just before lunch! This is where the term Renaissance Man came from: the ability to turn your hand to almost anything cultured.

LEONARDO DA VINCI (1452–1519)

Now there's clever, and there's very clever, and then there's Leonardo – who practically invented the word. He was born the illegitimate son of a lawyer from Vinci, a little town near Florence. Recognizing that his boy was no slouch when it came to drawing, Mr da Vinci sent young Leo to be an apprentice with Verrocchio, the famous painter/sculptor just up the road.

In those days there were no art schools, but instead a bright kid would learn how to do it by helping his boss (the artist), washing out the paint pots, mixing colours, filling in the big areas and nipping out to get the wine, bread and olives for lunch. Many would have it (including me) that as a way of learning basics and earning your dues, so to speak, that was a far better system than what we have now, but now is not the time to go into that.

So young Leonardo was happy as a kid in a sweet factory carving up rocks, making things out of metal, delving into human anatomy, pulling plants to bits, mixing colours, learning perspective and examining everything around him in its minutest detail.

Let's face it, most brightish kids would have done OK in that environment, but being an embryonic genius shoved our lad well ahead of the bunch. Soon everyone was talking about the boy from Vinci and before long, he left Verrocchio and set up on his own with his own little helpers.

Leonardo da Vinci
St John the Baptist
1513–16

What makes Leonardo so valuable to us Art Historians (who am I kidding?) is that he wrote everything he ever did or thought in his notebooks. Unfortunately it's in back-to-front mirror writing; not, I must stress, because he couldn't do it the right way round but, more likely, because he didn't want his ideas pinched by every Tom, Dick or Luigi. Seriously, it was more likely that his ultra-modern ideas were so radical that he could well have been had up for heresy if they'd gotten in front of the wrong people.

You see, Leonardo never believed anything that he couldn't actually check out with his own eyes and investigations. Nothing or nobody was safe in his workshops. He chopped up at least thirty ex-Italians and whole zoosful of animals and birds just to find out how they worked (or used to!).

He became so mega-famous that everyone who was anyone up Italy way wanted to enhance their own status by having him work for them. On the negative side, whether it was for the cash or the fame or sheer curiosity, Leonardo became known for taking on more work than he could possibly do, and therefore hardly ever finishing anything. To be honest I'd have been well hacked off if I'd spent a load of my hard-earned lire and ended up with a half-painted front room, Leonardo or not. But, being recognized as a universal genius, he could get away with murder.

In painting, his major contribution was the development of chiaroscuro, which involved putting down the whole composition in the tones of one single colour to start with. Boring, you might think, but the reason for doing this was to enable the artist to balance the tonal values before getting the colours out, a method later copied by painters like Caravaggio and Rembrandt.

His most famous painting, and probably *the* most famous painting ever, was called the *Mona Lisa,* which can be seen on T-shirts, tin trays and postcards throughout the world. I've always been a bit puzzled as to its huge success. OK, it's a nice bit of

brushwork, but no better than lots of other stuff around at the time; and Miss Lisa was certainly no great looker. That huge black frock she wore could have hidden just about anything.

The secret seems to be in her expression. For centuries the world has wondered just what was on her mind as her chum Leo was doing her portrait. Some think she was hiding a little smile, others believe it was covering a deep sadness (and she was putting a brave face on it), while yet others believe she was well fed up and just couldn't wait to get home to put the old pasta on for all the little Lisas. For all we know those fingers on her right hand could have been frozen in the act of drumming impatiently.

Leonardo must have known this confusion would occur, for he used a method of painting called *sfumato,* which cleverly involved blurring the corners of the eyes and mouth, or hiding them in shadow, so that the expression and mood could be left to interpretation. Beyond that, however, Leonardo finally cracked the ancient problem of portraiture: to show something beyond just the physical representation of his subjects' faces. He let them live.

As if all this wasn't enough, Leonardo found time to explore many aspects of science like the mysteries of the human body, how waves and currents work, and how insects and birds get about in the air. It's generally accepted that he first discovered that a machine resembling a helicopter would one day fly.

M. BUONARROTI (1475–1564)

If you're wondering why you've never heard of this other all-time great, don't worry. He's much better known by his Christian name – Michelangelo. His upbringing and early training were much like that of Leonardo's, being apprenticed to Domenico Ghirlandaio, a popular painter whose fashionableness rather got in the way of long-lasting acclaim. There he learned every aspect of painting, sculpting and drawing and also gained a love of things scientific. By the time he was ready to go it alone, there wasn't a single drawing problem he couldn't handle. In fact, the more difficult it was, the more Michelangelo liked it. By the time he was thirty he shared top artist billing with Leonardo, his old 'rival', and the phone never stopped ringing with enticing requests for his talent.

Michelangelo's life didn't run as smoothly as Leonardo's, however, and he was often getting into severe Pope trouble, particularly with Julius II who kept changing his mind about what he wanted him to do. One minute he had Michelangelo quoting on sculpting what would be the tomb to die for, and then, just as he was getting into the idea, Julius went off it. Michelangelo was so cross he sent him a very rude letter which was, apparently, a rather dangerous thing to do, Popewise, in those days.

Luckily Julius needed him more than he needed Julius, so Michelangelo was forgiven and asked to paint the Pope's ceiling. Now this might not seem much to us – a couple of coats of magnolia (silk finish) usually does the trick – but in those days Popes usually went in for something a little more, how would you say, fancy – and that's just what Julius ended up with.

Michelangelo *The Libyan Sibyl* (from the Sistine Chapel ceiling) 1511

Michelangelo shocked everyone by locking himself away in the Sistine Chapel for over four years and painting, on his back (no! not the Pope's back), the most ornate and awe-inspiring ceiling ever seen. It is said that when he'd finished, he was so used to craning his neck upwards that he couldn't read a letter unless he held it above his head.

But Michelangelo's true love was sculpture and he is remembered as much for his carving as anything else. Julius eventually gave him the go-ahead to do his tomb, but by that time he was knackered, and never got round to finishing it.

One later criticism of the great man's work stems from the knowledge that he only liked men. He, therefore, only represented the opposite sex with bits added on and one particular bit taken off.

RAPHAEL (1483–1520)

Raphael *Nymph of Galatea c.*1514

While Michelangelo and Leonardo were battling it out in Florence in 1504, a young chap called Raphael Sanzio turned up with a reference from his old boss Perugino (leader of the Umbrian school and a famous painter in his own right, churning out hundreds of sweet Madonnas and grumpy Jesuses – reproductions of his work can be seen on just about every parlour wall in the Catholic world). Anyway, the letter basically said that young Raphael was 'the business', artwise. Anyone else would have packed up their kit and become scarce when he'd realized the standard that had been set by the big boys Leonardo and Michelangelo, but Raphael wasn't put off and even flourished, probably because he wasn't nearly as stroppy as the other two.

Raphael eventually went to Rome just as Michelangelo was climbing the ladder to paint the Pope's ceiling. Talk about timing. The Pope was looking for someone to do the Vatican walls and the young painter just happened to knock at the door on the right day. The beauty of this work must be seen to be believed.

A typical Raphael painting of this period is the *Nymph of Galatea,* which rather suggests a scene from an early Roman blue movie. Nymphs and sea gods romp willy-nilly, while porky cherubs, who seem not to like the young miss from Galatea, wheel about threatening her with their bows and arrows. One of them seems to have run right out of steam and appears to be clinging for dear life to the front of what looks like a pedalo.

Unlike his Italian Cinquecento contemporaries, Raphael, obviously a bit of a crawler, went in for flattering and idealizing his subjects. Therefore, if you want to see what the general public thought was sexy back in the fifteenth century, flick through Raphael's paintings. I don't think they'd make Italian *Playboy* these days, however.

Other Great High Renaissance Names to Drop

Nobody, I'm afraid, held a candle to the three big names.

CHAPTER 13

Meanwhile, Up Venice Way

The Early Sixteenth Century

We haven't mentioned what was going on in Venice while art in Florence blossomed. The bottom still hadn't fallen out of the Madonna and child market and Jacopo Bellini with his two lads Gentile and the soon to be famous Giovanni ran the family firm producing various Virgins, portraits for the Venetian state and work for Venetian charitable organizations. The three of them must be credited with the birth of the Venetian school of painting. Hardly anything remains of poor old Jacopo's work and Gentile, who took over the business when Dad died, was sent off by the government to Istanbul to work for Sultan Mehmet II (which seems a bit cheeky). Gentile's (slightly the worse for wear) portrait of his new boss hangs in London's National Gallery.

GIOVANNI BELLINI (1433–1516)

Giovanni stayed home and perfected the Netherlandish method of using oil paint in glazes rather than egg yolk. Unlike Leonardo, he showed perspective and depth by alternating wedges of light and dark colour from foreground to background, a technique soon to be ripped off by many successive landscape painters. His *Madonna With Saints* is a fab example of his mastery of light and colour, although it must be said that, to my eye, his figures seem just a little plastic, especially young Jesus who looks as if he could be Barbie and Ken's vacuum-moulded offspring. Bellini's workshop was even more remarkable, however, for the amount of talent that flowed from it, throwing out such masters as Giorgioni and the late, great Titian.

Giovanni Bellini *St Francis in Ecstasy* c.1485

TITIAN (1477–1576)

Titian was to become as famous as Mike and Leo were in Florence. True, he wasn't as versatile as them, or as popular as Mr Nice Guy Raphael. Instead he just worked away day by day, week by week, refining and perfecting his painting technique, reaching a standard that was seldom to be equalled. In his *Madonna With Saints*, the young Jesus seems at last like a real crying, laughing and everything else-ing baby. The lady that's 'playing' the Virgin Mary, on the other hand, looks a bit worn out, as if she's dying to give the awkward little varmint to some saint or other while Titian gets on with the painting.

But forget all the religious stuff; Titian was the guy for portraits. He was able to get to the same place as all the Leonardos and Raphaels with half the effort and a quarter of the brushstrokes,

Titian *Bacchus and Ariadne c.*1480

achieving a reality and sensitivity that equalled and often outstripped everything that had gone before.

Everyone who was anyone queued up to have their picture done, and *not* because the master flattered them. Far from it, in those long-lost days before photography, Titian achieved the sort of realism that led the customers to believe that through the warts-and-all honesty of their portraits they might achieve some kind of eternity. Titian didn't have it all his own way, however, as he died tragically aged ninety-nine in 1576 from a nasty bout of plague. Mind you, being Italian, he wouldn't have got a telegram from the Queen anyway.

CORREGGIO (1494–1534)

Florence and Venice were definitely the hot spots for all the arts, but up in northern Italy, in the little town of Parma, a quiet painter called Antonio Allegri, better known as Correggio (after the town he came from), was developing a unique painting style loosely based on that which Leonardo had introduced a few years before. Leonardo and Raphael had, by this time, gone to join all those trillions of angels and cherubs that seemed to fill the Italian skies, Michelangelo was now a bit past it, and Titian had become very much the top man.

Correggio's almost cinematic use of single-source lighting and deep shadows was copied by generations of painters who never seemed to quite get it right. In his painting *Holy Night*, young Jesus positively glows from the crib like those silly plastic duck lamps, lighting up the whole manger, while the statutory few angels flit around in the roof like moths round a candle. St Joseph stands, meanwhile, outside doing something we can't quite see with his ass. Correggio's great speciality, however, became painting ceilings in churches to look as if they weren't really there. During the interminable services the flock loved to be able to look straight up to what appeared to be the dazzling heavens, though there were quite a few objections to the views up the angels' frocks. You obviously, even then, couldn't please all the people all the time. Maybe they were Mary Whitehouse's ancestors.

Correggio *Holy Night c.*1530

Germany and the Netherlands

So it's fair to say that things were going along quite nicely in Italy at the beginning of the sixteenth century. But what about north of the Alps? Things weren't nearly so happy. For a start their rather crude Gothic style was beginning to get on everyone's nerves, and they were becoming fed up with looking longingly southwards for any kind of progress in learning or art. How come the Italians had perfected the rendering of the human body? Why could they use perspective so freely and accurately? And why did their buildings have such a classical grace, compared to the Gothic piles they were still putting up at home?

The latter only started to change when the princes and well-to-dos who'd spent many a holiday in the Italian sunshine decided their status would be much improved if they pinched all these 'new' ideas when commissioning new buildings. Unfortunately, the northern European architects took a long time to get the hang of it, tending to design the same old stuff as before, but tarting them up with a few classical columns here, and a few pretty mouldings there. The results, though often having a quirky charm about them, missed the point completely, causing visiting Italian architects great amusement (those who ever bothered to venture north).

It was similar with painting. Northern artists just couldn't get the hang of the 'new' style. All except a young artist in Germany, the son of a Hungarian master goldsmith.

ALBRECHT DÜRER (1471–1528)

Young Albrecht was what was commonly known as a child prodigy, displaying a capacity for drawing far ahead of his years. He was apprenticed with the busiest woodcut and engraving workshops in Nuremberg but eventually left for Basle in Switzerland which was the European centre for book production. From there he travelled extensively in Italy with his sketch book and studied the art of the greats, particularly Mantegna – his favourite. When he returned to Nuremberg he married a very grumpy wife and opened his own workshop. It became clear very soon that he was not any old working draughtsman, but in fact a great artist, and he became the first German to know and teach the rules of perspective and the proper proportions of the human body.

Albrecht Dürer *Lot and his Daughters* 1498

His favourite subject (probably because of his wife) was the end of the world, or Doomsday, which, though not exactly a barrel of laughs, tickled the fancy of a Germany bored rigid with its Church. In fact many of his audience really believed Albrecht's visions of the end of the world and thought it could well happen in their lifetime.

Dürer was honoured and loved by all his contemporaries and became the major influence on German art.

Nothing much was happening in the Netherlands at this time. Like their neighbours the Germans, they were struggling with an uneasy cross between the tired old stuff that dated from the Middle Ages and the new images and ideas from Italy, until . . .

HIERONYMUS BOSCH (1455–1516)

Although very little is known about Mr Bosch, he is generally accepted to be the greatest (and weirdest) Dutch painter of the period. Strangely enough, he wouldn't have the 'new' style in the house, preferring to use the old-fashioned but very realistic method to portray terrifying events that no human eye had seen before.

Hieronymus Bosch *The Lure of Folly c.*1500

Yet Bosch was a highly religious and highly moral man, so he delighted in showing his often terrified audience what could happen to one if one wasn't. If you like arms and legs being torn out of their sockets, sinners being boiled alive in cauldrons of oil, or being eaten by half-man, half-lizardy-type monsters, only to be excreted out in the most undignified manner, then old Hieronymus is the boy for you. His *Garden of Earthly Delights* (which I think might be a sort of Dutch joke) is obviously his idea of hell and I must say really looks no fun at all (even worse than Alton Towers) and certainly stands as a lesson to all of us who don't finish up our greens.

Bosch has had considerable influence on many modern surrealist painters, animators and illustrators, not just because of the horror of his imagery, but the incredible way he let his imagination run riot. Brilliant stuff!

Other Early Sixteenth-century Artists' Names to Drop

Giorgione, Grünewald, Cranach, Altdorfer.

CHAPTER 14

Mind Your Mannerisms

Later Sixteenth-century Art

I should think that if you were, or wanted to be, a painter around 1520 in Italy, you'd be a bit fed up. The general feeling was that art, as such, had gone just about as far as it possibly could. The great masters, like Leonardo and Michelangelo, had really rung the bell, perfection had been reached, and there was very little point trying to do anything except be as good as them as was humanly possible. Their draughtsmanship combined with perspective, applied to just about any subject you like, treated to a huge dollop of harmony and correctness, had sure made them a class act.

There followed a rather strange, lost period where the painters of the day would simply copy the great nudes of Michelangelo, for instance, and compose their religious scenes around them. The result often looked like a cross between an ecclesiastical nudist camp and a rather gay athletic training session. This style was to become known as Mannerism, owing to its lavish attention to stylization.

A few of these Mannerists, however, thought they could out-do the old masters. After all it was Leonardo himself who said, rather smugly I think, that it was a wretched student who couldn't surpass his master. Considering he was perhaps the finest draughtsman (drawer) that ever lived, it was a bit of an empty challenge. Talk about rubbing their poor noses in it! Nevertheless these painters, rather than try to out-draw the old-timers (sounds like a Western!), decided to make their imagery less obvious, less simple and, if you like, less simply, obviously, beautiful.

A good example of this can be seen in Parmigianino's Madonna, known as the *Madonna with the Long Neck*. It was quite the thing in those days to elongate the human form purely for effect,

Parmigianino *The Madonna with the Long Neck* 1535

and Parmigianino really tugged out the poor Virgin's neck so that she resembled one of those loony African women who shove loads of rings round theirs to make them longer. In fact, had she stood up I reckon she could have got a place in an all-girl college basketball team, as she looks at least six foot eight inches tall!

Although a lot of these Italians' paintings seem rather amusing today, they'd have made Mike and Leo turn in their tombs. The mere fact that they were trying to move away from anatomically correct, harmonious representation of nature and the human body often gives them the label of the first 'modern' artists, but I'll personally save that 'honour' till later. But they didn't all fail, for in Venice there was a young artist called Jacopo Robusti who was carving a great name, or rather nickname, for himself.

TINTORETTO (1518–94)

Tintoretto *The Origin of the Milky Way* 1570s

Jacopo Robusti, or Tintoretto (nicknamed after his father, a dyer), had become rather bored with the calm beauty of his predecessor Titian's paintings and, although admitting to finding them pleasing, reckoned they lacked a certain emotion or passion. He certainly gave his work that, sacrificing beauty and immaculate finish for swashbuckling movement. Tintoretto wasn't one to spend ages over a painting: he often abandoned it as soon as he thought it had made its religious point.

EL GRECO (1541–1614)

El Greco *Christ Driving the Traders from the Temple* 1600

Meanwhile from the island of Crete (where it all started) came a young man called Domenikos Theotokopoulos. They called him El Greco (The Greek) as his real name must have made him sound more like a kebab-house owner than a painter. Even so, he was actually the first painter from that neck of the woods to produce anything of any note since the Dark Ages (not that Greece actually *had* been dark for ages). He saw nothing particularly exciting in the 'new' Italian style and, more to the point, wasn't in the least bit shocked by Tintoretto's brash, passionate and often moving paintings. Like Tintoretto, he wanted to tell the great religious stories as he believed they happened, full of movement and excitement. After refining his art in Venice he took himself off to Toledo in Spain, probably so that he wouldn't have critics telling him off every five minutes.

He went much further than Tintoretto in his disregard for natural, realistic forms and colours, producing lopsided compositions and even stretched figures like Parmigianino. Somehow, however, his didn't look pretentious or overworked. El Greco was, however, a cocky so-and-so. Once, in Rome, there was a debate in the Papal court as to whether Michelangelo's *Last Supper* should be demolished because it contained nudity. The Greek let it be known that if it was destroyed he would paint a much better one.

Today, his stuff looks strangely 'modern', but it's fair to say that his Spanish audience didn't bat an eyelid even though they'd seen nothing like it before (and probably because they were too busy fighting the English). Unfortunately it took only a generation for the 'sophisticated' art-buying public to start taking the mickey out of his unnatural imagery, and then it took till well after the Second World War, centuries later, for poor El to be appreciated as one of the sixteenth century's, if not history's, greatest painters. Could *he* be the father of modern art? Watch this space.

Other Great Mannerist Names to Drop

Pontormo, Fiorentino, Savoldo, Bronzino.

CHAPTER 15

Art or Not

Northern Europe, Sixteenth Century

It was fine for all those painters down in Italy and Spain. The only thing they had to think about was how to make their work look new and exciting. Up in Germany, Holland and England it was a different picture altogether. The real debate was whether there should be any painting at all!

After the Reformation most of these newfangled Northern European Protestants reckoned that those angel-filled altarpieces, and statues of saints and things, were nothing but Popish idol worship. The stricter ones even made out that any sort of interior decoration, like the odd fresco or decorated ceiling, was silly frivolity and not to be encouraged. Having said that, the buildings that were being built around that period were so gloomy that even the jolliest Laura Ashley wallpaper wouldn't have cheered them up.

So the poor painter's work was cut down to crummy old book illustration, or the odd non-smiley portrait (fun was banned). It was a bit like a talented architect only being allowed to do loft conversions.

HANS HOLBEIN THE YOUNGER (1497–1543)

Hans Holbein the Younger was, strangely enough, the son of Hans Holbein the Elder, a successful German painter. Young Hans had been doing really well, painting and drawing in a style that, though unmistakably Northern, showed a real understanding of the major principles of the Italian Renaissance.

After working in Basle, Switzerland, where everything was still where it was at culture-wise, he decided to move even further afield,

Hans Holbein *Jean de Dinteville and George de Selve 'The Ambassadors'* 1533

and with a letter of recommendation from Erasmus, the well-known Swiss scholar and all-round clever person, he turned up in London to see Sir Thomas More. More, as we all know, eventually got the cruellest chop from King H. VIII, but our Hans got on fine with the bad King Henry and eventually became the court painter. It obviously meant no more Virgins and Jesuses so, as well as doing just about everyone important's portrait, he designed everything from furniture to jewellery, court costumes to goodness knows what else – all around the various palaces.

His early portraits had lots of off-the-subject detail, to the point where it could be said that he was simply showing off his ridiculous technical skill. His later (and better) ones, however, had plain, simple backgrounds giving far more emphasis to the sitter.

On a slightly sadder note, Hans Holbein perished in the plague of 1543, and a large part of his work went up in flames in the Great Fire of 1666. Maybe he should have stayed home.

PIETER BRUEGEL (1525–69)

The only Protestant country in Northern Europe to see a way through the strangling effects of the Reformation on art was the Netherlands, whose artists decided to concentrate on the sort of stuff to which the Church could have no objection. OK there was no denying that the Italians had the representation of humans in motion licked, but when it came to painstaking observation and the rendering of nature – be it a leaf, a tree, or even a herd of cows – in perfect detail, those Flemings had the world beat. Like other Protestant artists, they got into severe trouble if they tackled anything vaguely religious, so they stuck to everyday scenes from everyday life.

Pieter Bruegel *The Peasant's Wedding* c.1568

By far the most famous of these recorders was Pieter Bruegel the Elder. He spent his life painting scenes of country life, to such a degree that for many years it was thought he must have been of common stock himself. Not a bit of it. Pieter Bruegel came from a posh family and sold his brilliant canvases to wealthy bankers and intellectuals. Even King Rudolph II bought many of his paintings, obviously getting off on seeing how the other half lived. But Bruegel wasn't laughing at them, or even being patronizing; his paintings showed great sympathy and even love for the simple Flemish countryman. If you want a Christmas card showing hardworking pleasant peasants, going about their business in decorative manner, then Bruegel's the boy to look for.

Other Sixteenth-century European Artists' Names to Drop

Nicholas Hilliard, Jan Goujon, Jacques Callot.

CHAPTER 16

All Back to Rome

Seventeenth-century Art

At around the same time as Guy Fawkes was beginning to tire of the Anglican Parliament, the art world was beginning to tire of Mannerism, but, as usual, was not sure of what they wanted to follow it. Rome was the centre of the operations, and it was there that all the intellectual arguments (yawn) about art began. Was painting better than sculpture? (Is an egg better than a tree?) Was design more important than colour? (Is sky more important than sea?) While all these pointless quarrels were going on, a brilliant young painter pitched up in Rome from Milan who had rejected Mannerism completely.

MICHELANGELO MERISI DA CARAVAGGIO (1571/3–1610) AND THE NATURALISTS

Let's face it, with a Christian name like that you couldn't go far wrong, and in most respects Caravaggio didn't. Unlike the other splendid painter, the Florentine Annibale Carracci, who was also working in Rome at the time, Caravaggio rejected the Italian habit of beautifying and romanticizing everything, regarding it as wimpish. He wanted to kick all that stuff out and start in a fresh, real and true-to-life way. His many critics regarded him as a sort of visual heathen, rejecting all that was beautiful in the world. He was labelled by them as a 'naturalist', which doesn't sound that much of an insult to me but apparently made Caravaggio – a well-known angry young man – fighting mad. Having said that the name stuck, and it started what was to become a well-known movement.

To be fair, all he ever wanted to do, being deeply religious,

Caravaggio *Young Bacchus c.*1600

was to portray all his favourite biblical scenes as he saw them in his head. No haloes, no skies full of angels, no chubby cherubs and no disciples or saints looking like they'd just finished a bodybuilding course. He tried to paint people as they really were and his use of light, influenced by the master of the one light bulb, Correggio, gave his later pictures an eerie intimacy and realism that has never, in the history of painting, been equalled.

But Caravaggio was regarded as a right rough boy by the public at large and, worse than that, a very bad sport. In 1606 he apparently fled Rome having killed his tennis partner over a dispute, probably a dodgy line call. He was severely injured himself but managed to reach Naples where, after being patched up, he continued his work.

Two years later he went to Malta to become a monk, but was hardly there for five minutes before he rubbed up the boss of the monastery the wrong way and, believe it or not, got himself banged up in a cell. He escaped the following year and dashed out some rather hasty canvases in Sicily. This all sounds like a movie!

Talk about rotten luck. When he returned to Naples a group of hired hoodlums left him badly disfigured having rearranged his face with their stilettos (*not* high-heeled shoes). As if this wasn't bad enough, when a little Italian bird told him that he was due for a pardon for the tennis murder that he was still running from, he set sail instantly and was then arrested (by mistake, as it turned out) at Port Ercole. While held there, he thought his belongings had disappeared with the ship that had just brought him (they were, in fact, still in the customs hall). Just as poor Caravaggio set out after them, he caught a horrid fever and died. He never got to hear about the pardon which had been granted a week earlier (and presumably never got his luggage back). A tragic end to an artist who is now recognized as one of the world's finest masters.

Both Carracci and Caravaggio fell way down the painting pop charts in the nineteenth century but recently, I'm happy to report, have soared to the top again.

NICOLAS POUSSIN (1594–1665)

Nicolas Poussin *The Adoration of the Golden Calf* c.1636

Nicolas Poussin was by far the most notable French painter of this period. He came to Rome when thirty and soon became one of the most respected 'academic' masters. His work was brilliant, if you like that sort of thing, but many people find his heavily idealized Roman landscapes (obviously painted indoors), half-clad portly shepherdesses and muscle-bound shepherds – all looking as if they'd been playing that game where you freeze when the music stops – a bit on the kitsch side.

PETER PAUL RUBENS (1577–1640)

Every bit as kitsch, but far more fun (and far more talented), this brilliant young painter came to Rome from the Netherlands in 1600. Rubens listened in on all the aforementioned, ear-numbing arguments about who did what, why and when in art, and studied closely the work of the Italian greats. When he returned to Antwerp aged thirty-one no one could touch him for pure draughtsmanship and use of colour anywhere north of the Alps.

One of his greatest gifts was the ability to render just about any material from the flimsiest gossamer to the shiniest steel with uncanny ease. Everything he touched was given instant vibrant life, from the huge set pieces, crammed with all the usual overweight cherubs, saints and virgins, to a simple sketch of a child.

Unlike the other Flemish painters, who fiddled around with little canvases, Rubens liked to work huge – which was just as well as the patrons of that time were a bit like many Japanese buyers are now. That is, they very often valued art on how big it was.

He still did his fair share of the good old Virgin and Child moneyspinner, but somehow, Rubens breathed life into them so that they didn't have that terrible static feel of a high street window display.

Everywhere you look in his *Betrothal of St Catherine* there's something really wacky going on. St Catherine herself, who later reckoned she was married to our Jesus (wishful thinking or what?), doesn't appear to have made it, which is just as well as poor Jesus is still just a nipper. Among the 'guests', however, is a very

Peter Paul Rubens *The Betrothal of St Catherine* 1628

snazzy-looking St George who has obviously seen fit to drag his dead dragon along. St Sebastian just beside him doesn't seem to have read the invitation properly, and looks like a rather camp strippergram, appearing completely naked, save for a strategically placed piece of cloth on which hangs a quiver full of arrows (ouch!). In the background two pesky young angels are doing something rather horrid to a lamb, while in the sky a lumpy cherub seems to be playing hoopla by trying to drop a wreath over Mary's head.

This wonderful sketch was typical of the sort of thing Rubens would drop into the hands of his many talented apprentices to take away and paint big. Rubens would get on with something else and then mosey along when they'd finished, to touch up the odd face or smooth out the folds of the odd frock. This way of working enabled the master to churn out more work than now appears to be humanly possible, to make more cash than practically any painter had done before and become as famous as any artist up to that time. He became so influential, in fact, that towards the end of his life he would travel in state from court to court sorting out quite tricky diplomatic problems.

But all this cannot take away from his astonishing talents as a draughtsman. Rubens was the master of joyous painting in which all the men look like American Gladiators and all the women large, pink and roly-poly (which, to be fair, was just how they liked them in those days). I personally prefer his preparation sketches, which demonstrate an incredible facility for loose brush drawing sometimes lost in the large, and often overworked, finished canvases.

ANTHONY VAN DYCK (1599–1641)

Hundreds of students must have passed through old Rubens' hands during his long career, but none more famous than Anthony van Dyck who, though twenty or so years junior to Rubens, belonged to the same era as Poussin and Claude Lorrain. He was obviously a bright kid, being a master by the age of nineteen, and having picked up many of his boss's tricks of the trade like how to render different materials perfectly. However, it seems that van Dyck was

Anthony van Dyck *Lady Elizabeth Thimbleby and Dorothy, Viscountess of Andover c.*1657

a bit of a gloomy, not very well, sort, which can be seen in his work and generally he is regarded as being less fun and far more sentimental than his ex-boss Rubens. Mind you most people were a bit gloomy in those days so he became rather popular, especially when, in 1632, he came over to London and became Sir Anthony van Dyck, court painter to Charles I. In his famous portrait of his new boss, Tony manages to flatter the king so much it makes you wince. This, of course, was brilliant for business and soon everyone wanted to be painted as they would like to be regarded by their peers.

Owing to this pressure of work, he had teams of assistants churning out 'factory' pictures. Van Dyck would usually do the heads and the hands, but left all the rest to his lads. They were so busy, apparently, that they had a sort of production line of dummies wearing the clothes of the latest sitters. This did nothing for the furtherance of portrait painting and it must be said as an epitaph to the great man that when van Dyck was good, he was truly great, but when he was bad he descended into the worst kind of stylized Mannerism and extreme superficiality.

DIEGO DE VELÁZQUEZ (1599–1660)

While on his holidays in Spain one year Rubens bumped into a young man who was born in the same year as his pupil van Dyck and was doing the same job for Philip IV, the Spanish king, as van Dyck was doing for Charles I over in England.

Velázquez had been bowled over by the work of Caravaggio, or should I say his 'naturalist' imitators. Even his early work showed the same disregard for convention and the same passion for intimate observation as his hero.

Rubens gave him a great tip when they met. He advised him to ask the king to give him permission to go over to Rome to study his heroes at first hand – which he did in 1630. On his

Diego de Velázquez *The Toilet of Venus* *c.*1648

return to Spain Velázquez executed a series of extremely gloomy portraits which were, nevertheless, to establish him as one of the great person-painters of all time.

While in Rome he'd looked really closely at the brushwork of Rubens and Titian and many believe he surpassed both of them. A good example is his wonderful painting of Pope Innocent X. Velázquez captures the broody, slightly sinister, almost cynical demeanour of a man who looks anything but innocent. There is a reality that travels through the centuries and the viewer realizes that despite the work of many of his contemporary portraitists the human face really hasn't changed at all. Many critics regard him as a better artist than van Dyck. That might be true for a lot of the stuff he did, but I think when van Dyck was really going for it, there was no one around to touch him.

Other Great Seventeenth-century Artists' Names to Drop

Guido Reni, Claude Lorrain, Georges de la Tour, Louis le Nain.

CHAPTER 17

Triple Dutch

Holland, Seventeenth Century

When Europe split between Catholics and Protestants in 1688 it had a great effect on European art, especially in the Netherlands. The south (Belgium) stayed Catholic, but the north (Holland) had had enough of being bossed about by the surly Spanish Catholics and decided to be Protestant. The boring northern folk didn't like the lively baroque style of the southern painters, preferring their art to be more sober and dignified. English and German art was still under the same Protestant boot that had squashed it back at the beginning of the seventeenth century and was still trying to find a way out. Painters continued struggling to find subjects that weren't going to raise the hackles of the religious 'mafia'.

FRANS HALS (1580–1666)

The first of the great Dutch masters of the period, Frans Hals, had moved up from the southern Netherlands to the prosperous Dutch city of Haarlem. His portraits broke completely new ground. Instead of the poor subject coming back, time after time, to sit for hours on end, you get the impression that Hals didn't hang about, and slapped the paint on as quick as possible. This gives his work a freshness and energy never seen before, almost like a brilliant impromptu snapshot. His clients must have been shocked at seeing themselves not as a mirror image, but as others saw them.

But it was all too much too quickly and poor Hals soon found he was way ahead of his time. He was breaking too many of the old established rules and, because he was frowned on by the wealthy art-buying public, he often had to flog his work for peanuts at local markets and cart-boot sales.

Frans Hals *Young Man Holding a Skull c.*1626

Unfortunately, in those days hardly anyone actually *asked* a painter for a picture; the poor devil would have to do one first and then try to get rid of it. On top of that he would have to specialize. Once a landscape painter, always a landscape painter; or once a portrait painter always a portrait painter.

All the same, poor Frans never made a bean out of painting and often had to beg for favours from local shopkeepers. He died penniless in an almshouse having been supported by a few of the governors whom he'd painted. Although many people tried to imitate Hals, no one really managed to get near his virtuosity. About the best of the bunch was a woman called Judith Leyster, though to give her even more credit, her work really paved the way for the great Jan Vermeer who wasn't to turn up for a generation.

Her career, like so many women painters before and since, was cut short by having to bring up nippers.

REMBRANDT VAN RIJN (1606–69)

The best Dutch artist of the time by far, and arguably the greatest portrait painter that ever lived, was the son of a rich miller from Leyden. A not-bad scholar, young Rembrandt was always sneaking off from proper lessons to draw and paint until one day he never came back. At twenty he went up to Amsterdam where, being a smart lad, he got himself discovered as a portrait painter, bought a nice house and, best of all, married a rich woman. So far so good.

Rembrandt *Hendrickje Stoffels in Bed* 1647

When Mrs van Rijn died, she left her hubby well set up, and for some time Rembrandt had the lot. He was rich, healthy and immensely popular as an artist. Then, for no obvious reason, Rembrandt's style went out of fashion (typical Dutch fickleness) and his fortunes gradually dwindled through the 1640s until his creditors put his house and his own wonderful art collection up for sale. He died leaving nothing but a few old painty clothes and the tools of his trade.

Surprisingly, we have a fine record of how the master appeared throughout his life, as, although nothing to write home about looks-wise, he painted one or two self-portraits every year until practically the end. We can therefore see the rise and fall of a truly great man. Seriously, his last portrait almost makes one cry at the spectacle of a broken genius who would never know how revered he would later become, or the pleasure he would give to his millions of fans.

But why was Rembrandt so very special? It must be his sincerity. He really got under the skin of his sitter in such a way that had never been seen before or, dare I say, since. As we look at his work we can go so much further than simply looking at the shapes, patterns and skin textures of his subject. Rembrandt began where Hals left off, delving into his 'victim's' personality and, without sounding yukky, soul. For me the difference between a Rembrandt and a Hals is the difference between a fast, inspired sketch and a deep thought-provoking insight into two real persons' minds, the sitter *and* the artist. He crystallized all that had been achieved so far in terms of painting technique, and then added a huge dollop of his own.

For me, Rembrandt rules – OK?

JAN VERMEER (1632–75)

Last of the great Dutch trio was Mr Vermeer, king of the perfect can't-see-the-brushstrokes painting method. He was born and lived all his days in Delft, although very little is known about his life, which tragically ended when he was forty-three, leaving very few

Jan Vermeer *Lady with Milk Jug* *c.*1665

paintings. Unlike Jan Steen, his contemporary, who painted wonderful scenes of rough, tough, jolly Dutch home-life, Vermeer's paintings were far more simple, peaceful and thoughtful. He invites the viewer to look again at everyday objects, which he painted with a precision and love that never laboured the point (or paint). His technique was impeccable and unbelievable, always subtle, but for some reason never slick nor ostentatious. To compare it with a photograph would be an insult, as no snap could ever explain light and space as Vermeer did. No photograph could achieve the interlocking shapes that give his picture such a 'modern' feel. This very 'modern-ness' could be the reason for his true qualities not being realized by the dopey Dutch until a mere century ago. Poor Vermeer was never that happy, however, owing to his slow production rate (forty paintings in all), and carelessly fathering eleven kids. He was always skint and died hopelessly in debt.

His work remained unknown outside Holland until he was discovered by French art critic Thoré-Burger in 1866.

Other Great Seventeenth-century Dutch Painters' Names to Drop

Simon Vlieger, Jan van Goyan, Jacob van Ruisdael, Willem Kalf.

CHAPTER 18

Don't Knock Baroque

The Seventeenth Century

Baroque was the name given to a style of art that came out as a reaction against the distortions and confusions of the highly stylized Mannerism. It promoted simplicity and a return to some of the ideals of romantic Renaissance classicism (the study of ancient Greeks). In other words a sense of real theatre designed to grab and involve the spectator. Since the high Renaissance (Mike, Leo and Raphael, etc.) we haven't mentioned much about sculpture, but we can't ignore one child prodigy discovered in Rome.

GIOVANNI LORENZO BERNINI (1598–1680)

Lorenzo Bernini was born around the same time as van Dyck and was to become as much a master in three dimensions as van Dyck became in two. Following the High Baroque style of artists like Rubens, his work was even more emotional and, theatrically speaking, way over the top. This was not to the taste of boring Northern Europeans, but the southerners lapped it up. In fact Bernini was never a great hit in any non-Catholic country, even though his style was copied, albeit tamely, throughout Europe.

Bernini was the master of intensity. It's safe to say that in the whole history of sculpture no one had attempted such a comprehensive range of expressions – from deepest agony to rollicking ecstasy. It would have been so easy for his faces to slip into *Spitting Image*-like caricature, but somehow Bernini always managed to stay the right side of the funny fence.

He even managed to inject life into simple fabrics even though they were only made of stone. Instead of them hanging limply, as was standard procedure, Bernini would have the chap's frocks swirl around, as if caught by a strong breeze, which all helped create the sense of excitement and movement which typified all his best work. If you're ever up Rome way, go and see a few of his wonderful fountains, particularly the Triton or the really out-to-lunch Four Rivers. Both were commissioned by Popes, who seemed to have a really big thing about running water. Bernini died in 1680, thus, by way of absolutely nothing, sharing his personal extinction date with the dodo.

GIOVANNI BATTISTA GAULLI (1639–1709)

If you ever have anyone called Gaulli coming round to your house to paint the ceiling, let him in! He, like dear old Correggio, really got off on the idea of painting a ceiling to look like it wasn't there. If you thought that Correggio was a bit OTT in 1526, then Gaulli went totally bananas a hundred and fifty years later. His ceiling in the Jesuit church, Il Gesui, in Rome defies belief. Saints and sinners pour through the 'hole' in the roof like confetti, while demons and bad angels slither down the walls, miserable at having been kicked out of heaven above (and who can blame them). Gaulli delighted in confusing the poor Roman congregation to the point that it was impossible for the poor souls to spot the join between reality and illusion.

Rococo

If Baroque was the style of the gutsy and flamboyant, then Rococo was its rather delicate and sissy daughter. The first (and arguably greatest) exponent of this new decorative art form was a young, precocious Venetian . . .

GIOVANNI TIEPOLO (1696–1770)

Tiepolo was the pupil of a rather run-of-the-mill painter called Lazzarini who set out on his own in the 1720s and was soon

Giovanni Tiepolo *The Procession of the Trojan Horse into Troy*

cleaning up throughout Europe, embellishing and decorating anything from villas to palaces for anyone who could stump up the dosh. He would paint all subject matter – Greek mythology, religious scenes, great moments in history – with the same gay colours and light, almost fluffy, touch.

He and his two sons, 'the Tiepolo firm', were soon to be known for their lightning speed and frightening bank balance, and although their critics often gave them 10/10 for effort they were loath to give more than 3/10 for content and artistic integrity. In fact history tells us that Tiepolo and his ilk heralded the end of the golden age of Italian painting.

A good example of the sort of stuff he painted was *Chronos Entrusting Cupid to Venus,* a snappy little picture in which we see a motheaten Chronos (who looks as if he got his wings from an Oxfam shop) offering a somewhat lumpy-looking, bowless and wingless Cupid to an extremely pale Venus – who seems to be wearing nothing but a pair of Marks & Spencer sandals (modesty or what?). The dove flying away in the foreground resembles a skinny chicken, while to Venus's left there is a disapproving-looking eagly thing. The colours, however, are vibrant yet subtle at the same time and the composition beautifully balanced. Tiepolo, despite his shortcomings, still deserved the title of the greatest Rococo painter and the last of the great masters of the Italian Grand Manner founded in the High Renaissance of the sixteenth century. Like Rubens, his quick oil sketches are something to die for. It's difficult to believe that anyone could ever have drawn that well.

FRANCESCO GUARDI (1712–93)

Not all the painters of the time were going down the Tiepolo road. In fact, it was his brother-in-law Francesco who was breaking new ground in the same city, Venice. He did use the same sort of Rococo colours but up till this time they had only been used by people-painters as opposed to places-painters. His views of Venice became extremely sought after, especially as, unlike Tiepolo's work, you didn't need a big wall to hang them on. As old Tiepolo's stuff got bigger and bigger, Guardi's got smaller and smaller until some of his pictures were no larger than matchboxes. (I bet they don't sell in Japan – they only like big pictures.)

It was these small drawings that were often the most interesting though, as Francesco was one of the very first to use a sort of painter's shorthand. He would put in the essential parts of a scene, then, with no more than a few light dabs of his brush, indicate just enough for the viewer to fill in the rest with his imagination. This method was to be echoed by the Impressionists hundreds of years later.

CANALETTO (1697–1768)

Giovanni Antonio Canal (Canaletto) was another Venetian 'veduto' (painter of views) who started out touring with his brother and dad painting theatrical scenery in Venice and Rome. After a while he split to paint his own pictures but soon discovered a gravy-train that was to make him loads of loot. He found that churning out local Venetian scenes for Northern European tourists was far more lucrative than painting the odd time-consuming masterpiece.

Canaletto really got his act together and before long was able

Antonio Canaletto *Venice*
1697–1768

to hire a studio full of assistants producing, with increasing rapidity, a series of superbly crafted panoramas, all in the most intricate detail. He is reckoned to be one of the first (like Vermeer) to use a camera obscura, a sort of primitive pinhole camera for projecting images on paper in order to trace round them.

At the height of Canaletto's fame he decided to have a stab at cracking the British art market, but after quite a promising start painting some fine London vistas, he tailed off into near obscurity. Stick to Italy, Giovanni!

Other Great Rococo Artists' Names to Drop

Fragonard, Watteau, Marie-Louise Vigée-Lebrun.

CHAPTER 19

Art Snobs

England (and France) in the Eighteenth Century

It really hadn't been a lot of fun being a painter in England after the Reformation in the early sixteenth century, and the victory of Protestantism. But that wasn't the end of it as the hyper-grumpy Puritans headed by Cromwell really put the tin lid on images, fun and luxury, to such an extent that the only painting that was safe from the wrath of God was portraiture (as long as no one smiled). Unfortunately, the bourgeoisie, who were the only people able to afford paintings, only tended to buy the work of well-known foreigners, like Holbein and van Dyck. The art-buying public were such snobs in those days (so what's changed?) that anyone who wasn't either Italian or famous worldwide was not worth spending non-earned cash on. You can imagine how the English painters felt, especially a brilliant young engraver who'd been stuck for years with illustrating books (me too!).

WILLIAM HOGARTH (1697–1764)

Young Bill was unashamedly commercial. He realized that if he couldn't beat them, he must join, or even outflank them. It dawned on him that the only subject (outside portraiture) that would loosen those Puritan purse strings would be the illustration of the rewards of virtue and the wages of sin. First he did a series called *The Harlot's Progress* in 1732 which described the rise and fall (if you'll pardon the expression) of an eighteenth-century hooker in Georgian London. These sold OK so he decided to do another lot called *The Rake's Progress* in which a young boy starts off well but (and let this be a lesson) because of his greed ends up in Bedlam, a hideous lunatic asylum of the time. Hogarth swiftly

William Hogarth
Shortly After the Marriage 1743

followed with *The Four Stages of Cruelty* in which another young lad who started by teasing his cat (and let this be another lesson) ended up murdering people.

Being a shrewd businessman, he realized there wasn't nearly enough loot in just selling the original paintings, so he turned them into engravings which he not only printed and published himself, but sold by subscription, at a fraction of the price of the originals. In those days without radio, telly or crap newspapers, everyone loved to see those less fortunate than themselves, in whatever shape or form came readily to hand. Hogarth was to make a small fortune from this enterprise.

Towards the end of his life it all went rather sour, as his work gained a political flavour which got him into heaps of trouble, and just as the flak really started flying poor William promptly had a paralytic stroke – and died in 1764. However, since human nature changes not, his work is still pretty popular on account of its sleazy content.

JOSHUA REYNOLDS (1723–92)

It took a generation to pass before a painter came along who did satisfy both the puritanical bourgeoisie and the artistic connoisseur. Joshua Reynolds spent the best part of his twenties cruising round Italy picking up handy hints from the works of the great masters of the Renaissance and antiquity. When he got back to England he quickly became very famous and, many believe, very pompous. When he became president of the first Royal Academy of Art he told all the eager students that they should believe in the rules of taste and the importance of authority in art (what would he have made of Jeff Koons? *see* p. 189).

Reynolds firmly believed that the only way to get anywhere in the art game (my word, not his) was to study the great masters (his words, not mine). His famous line at his third RA discourse went like this: 'Instead of endeavouring to amuse mankind with the minute neatness of his imitations, the genuine painter must endeavour to improve them by the grandeur of his ideas.' Nice one, Josh!

Having said all this, though not in the same league as, say, Velázquez in paint handling, Reynolds showed great depth and personality in his portraits. Many think he lapsed far too often into chocolate-boxism, especially in paintings like *Miss Bowles With Her Dog*. The 'charming' subject looks like butter wouldn't melt in her cute little mouth (or the dog's for that matter), so much so that the painting reminds me of those horrendous portraits that high street photographers

Joshua Reynolds *Miss Bowles With Her Dog* 1755

do of kids, in which the fresh-scrubbed little darlings bear no resemblance to the little monsters that Mummy brought in. Many of his pictures have faded badly because Reynolds, so intent on telling everyone else what to do, was often very careless in the way he mixed his own paint. Reynolds himself faded badly in 1792.

Mind you, if you do like the sort of paintings you get on toffee tins or the birthday cards you buy for your granny then there was another painter who surpassed even Reynolds in sentimentalism.

THOMAS GAINSBOROUGH (1727–88)

To be fair, Gainsborough wasn't always going on about the great masters like Reynolds was. He was a 'natural' – a Suffolk country boy, who never thought it necessary to go to Rome, Florence or anywhere else foreign, for that matter. He picked all his skills up as he went along. It has to be said that although he was incredibly popular throughout the ages, many often find his portraits sickly to the point of wanting to throw up. His backgrounds are so idealized that they look like the scenery from a bad panto. Any minute you expect Puss-in-Boots to come out of the wings. He

Thomas Gainsborough *Mr and Mrs Andrews* 1750

even admitted that his landscapes paid little attention to accuracy or nature but were more 'carefully arranged to reflect mood'. Gainsborough was undoubtedly a brilliant technician, but then so was Tretchikoff who painted all the kitsch green-faced ladies in the 50s and 60s.

Both Reynolds and Gainsborough spent most of their lives fed up with having to churn out endless portraits of the rich and famous in order to make a living. But what a living! They would have loved to paint a few landscapes and still lifes, but neither was prepared to go hungry for it. Mind you, life could have been worse: in the year Gainsborough died, the first British convicts were sent off to Australia.

ANGELICA KAUFFMAN (1741–1807)

Angelica was born in Switzerland and eventually came to England with her dad, where she became one of the trendy painters of London society. Reynolds thought she was the bee's knees and helped her a lot with contacts. She eventually married an Italian painter and went home with him to Rome where she became the *grande dame* of the snobby Roman artistic society.

JEAN-BAPTISTE-SIMÉON CHARDIN (1699–1779)

It was during the eighteenth century that English institutions and taste became admired throughout Europe. English artists were catering far more for the general public (and painting them) as opposed to the glorification of a handful of rich fat-cat rulers. In France, too, the rather lumbering Baroque style was giving way to the more delicate Rococo; and more important than that, painters were beginning to look at ordinary folk for their subject matter, replacing all the gods, Popes and posh folk that had gone before.

By far the greatest painter of the period, up France way, was Chardin, who painted exquisite, almost Dutch-looking, pictures of everyday people doing everyday things. He was, however, to be

Jean-Baptiste-Siméon Chardin *The Young Schoolmistress* 1740

remembered for his fab still lifes. You know the sort of thing: 'casually' placed objects like fruit, wine, the odd lobster or dead bunny piled on a white tablecloth against a roughly plastered wall. These kinds of paintings were all the rage throughout Europe in those days and are still fetching huge prices today.

CHAPTER 20

Old Art in the Modern World

Neo-classicism: Late Eighteenth Century

It is always reckoned the world became modern when, in 1492, Christopher Columbus went on the longest boat trip of all to look for India, and rather fortunately (debatably) discovered America. This event heralded a very important period in art. It was known that the Renaissance had set adrift the painter and sculptor from mere mortals with ordinary jobs. It was also recognized that the Reformation, which followed, had put its Protestant shackles on art all over non-Catholic Europe, forcing artists to switch subject matter if they wanted to make an honest buck.

The ones who had kept going stuck to their guilds and companies, using apprentices in much the same way as would a plumber or a chef. As ever, they relied totally for their daily bread on the rich and royal, who really only saw art as a way of tarting up their palaces and castles, or as a way of achieving some sort of immortality through the sort of portraits that made them look dead important (when dead).

In short, artists were seen merely as suppliers of beautiful things to rich wasters with more money and time than they knew what to do with. The only real argument was the interpretation of what actually was beautiful. Some saw beauty in the 'Naturalisti' work of guys like Caravaggio or the Dutch painters; while others preferred the 'idealizers' like Reynolds and Gainsborough, and some even stuck fast to the old-timers like Raphael or Carracci.

The argument wasn't that heated, however, as the gulf between the three camps was not that great. After all, they all agreed that a 'proper' artist should study nature, the human form (*sans* clothes), and classical antiquity.

The Age of Reason

This way of thinking started to crumble around the back end of the eighteenth century, when the French became revolting and a whole load of assumptions about what was the right or wrong way to do things were brought out, dusted down and reassessed. This period became known as the Age of Reason and it brought with it a new self-consciousness and a re-examination of 'style' and 'styles'. Architects, particularly in Britain, started to question why every building had to look Palladian (temple-like) – all columns, porticoes and pediments. Why couldn't their clients choose what they wanted, like you would a new frock or different wallpaper? Why, couldn't they start looking back at the old Gothic style or, even better, the original Greek style that had been so bastardized over the centuries? Come to that, why couldn't they even build in the Chinese style that was becoming all the rage?

I wonder if the trouble with Chinese architecture was like what they say about Chinese food: a short while after you'd built something, you'd probably want something more substantial.

All over Europe the Rococo and Baroque styles were rejected as symbols of bourgeois aristocracy or stuck-up royalty, and in their place came a new wave which culminated in the Regency period of Neo-Classicist architecture (1810–1820), which created Greek-temple-type buildings with windows. It's interesting to note that 1812 was the year the British nicked the Elgin Marbles off the Greeks. In painting and sculpture the rift with tradition was not quite as straightforward. The apprenticeship system was on the way out and, to replace it, academies of art were sprouting up in Paris and London. Art students, as we know and love them, were born.

This was all very well, but having academies churning out loads of bushy-tailed, highly talented ex-students every five minutes only works if there are enough buyers to support them (it's exactly the same today). The trouble was that the art-buying public of the time were still only buying recognized masters (also the same today) and seldom took a chance on a newcomer.

Probably, like most of the collectors, then and now, they couldn't back their own judgement. So what could the academies do to attract the customer? They decided to have exhibitions of their students', and eventually more established artists', work in order to give the patron a choice.

These were the first public shows of art ever and they were to become the greatest social occasions of the time. Anybody who was anyone would attend, which made these exhibitions a fine (and profitable) new showcase for individual artists. But all good things have a negative side. As soon as the artists realized that they had to compete against each other on the same walls, they started to try to make their work more ballsy than their neighbours'. Hence they made their paintings as spectacular, colourful and downright big as possible, often to the detriment of quality. Surprise, surprise, many artists with more than a little integrity rebelled against these new exhibitions and 'academic' art in general.

New Subjects

Far more important than all this, however, artists felt themselves released from the need to paint the same old stuff as they'd always done before. Instead of religious scenes, Greek legends or the antics of various saints, they felt free to do what they fancied: a scene from a classical play, a great event in public life, anything that might catch the imagination of the buying public (and open their purses). Strangely enough the lead came from a group of expatriate American artists like John Singleton Copley (1738–1815) who, having polished up their technique in Europe, had set up their easels over this side of the pond. Typical of Americans, having no real tradition to fall back on, this lot saw no reason to get into all that old-fashioned stuff. They therefore started painting fairly controversial scenes from recent history – famous murders, arguments in parliament, anything that would sell – a bit like the tabloid newspapers do now. As day follows night, there was a strong reaction from the Establishment, who didn't want its dirty linen washed in public – reminiscent of the more recent hue and cry when it was announced that Parliament was to be televised.

JACQUES-LOUIS DAVID (1748–1825)

Meanwhile, back in La France, the French Revolution spawned a whole new batch of Neo-Classical artists. The revolutionaries saw themselves pretentiously as reincarnations of the Greek and Roman heroes. David as 'official artist' of the revolutionary government, and his paintings were often very political. His most famous work was of Marat, one of the leaders of the Revolution, a well-known good egg and 'friend of the people', lying dead in his bath. It appears Marat rather liked working wet and, as we see from the painting, had a kind of makeshift desk straddled across the tub. Apparently this rather odd French woman had an appointment with him (not *in* the bath!) as she wanted him to sign a petition. He obviously wasn't a friend of *all* the people for, just as he was about to stick his name on it, she stabbed him to death (which I think sounds a little ungrateful). It all seems such a long way from the

Jacques-Louis David *The Death of Marat* 1793

'charming' *Miss Bowles and Her Dog* by Reynolds, but was, all the same, just as great a hit.

FRANCISCO DE GOYA (1746–1828)

Another great painter to move away from tradition was the Spanish painter Goya. Not for him the revival of classicism, instead he tended to follow the painting style of Velázquez, the other famous Spanish artist. Like Velázquez he was determined not to flatter his portrait subjects. On the contrary, he seemed to delight in bringing out their worst qualities which, I'd have thought, in those pre-*Spitting Image* days, must have been a risky business. The trail of grumpy but brilliant court paintings he left behind him are made more amazing by the fact that he got away with them.

His portrait of the King of Spain, Ferdinand VIII, for instance, makes the sitter (or stander) look like a semi-moronic, hopelessly inbred but rather arrogant aristocrat (which no doubt he was). How interesting when we compare it with the spectacularly sycophantic official canvases of our Queen by slick, almost kitsch painters like Annigoni. You'd think with an art collection like hers,

Francisco de Goya *The Third of May 1808* 1814–15

she might know someone who could do a half-decent one. Or what about the series of photographic portraits by the royal photographer Norman Parkinson of Princess Anne, in which she looked like a cross between an upper-class bimbo and a *Vogue* model. (Nice one, Norm!)

As well as these wonderfully honest portraits, Goya was equally famous for his way-ahead-of-their-time etchings – the first to show areas of tone, as well as the customary fine lines. The subject matter of these prints was weird to say the least: demons, ghosts and witches, not from any religious preconceptions or obscure folklore, but straight from his own vivid (and slightly peculiar) imagination. Closer study reveals that Goya was obsessed with showing up the power and stupidity of the oppression that the ordinary Spaniard had suffered from so much in history. Like the Dutch painter Hieronymus Bosch over two hundred years before, he was one of the first to put the weird things that were churning round in his head on canvas for all to see.

WILLIAM BLAKE (1757–1827)

If Goya was a man with a message, then William Blake was so full of obscure messages that most of the art-buying public thought he was totally off his trolley. Blake, a South London boy, was deeply into religion and was often only kept from starvation by the few who recognized a talent different from anything that had ever been seen before.

Like Goya, he thought the art establishment a bunch of pompous prats, and would have nothing to do with the Neo-classicists (the pro-Greek and -Roman guys). His strange pictures, taken straight from his gloomy head as opposed to studies from life, bore a strange resemblance to the much later imagery of the hippie period. Most of his output was for books surrounding and accompanying his rather wacky poetry. Blake was often confused as to where his visions ended and reality began. For instance, he sometimes saw the image of an old naked man (probably God) measuring the globe with a huge compass, hovering at the top of his stairs in his Lambeth house. There is, I must add, no record

William Blake *Satan Smiting Job with Sore Boils* 1826

of Blake enjoying the pleasures of the bottle before going to bed (or God ever going to Lambeth).

At the time, his one-man revolt against the revelations of the Renaissance shocked his contemporaries. Who could have guessed, at the time, that history was to write him down as one of the greatest and most original figures in English art?

Landscapes in England

It was around this time, and in direct contrast to what Blake was into, that landscape painting came from backstage and caught the spotlight. Up to this time, making pretty pictures of the countryside was frowned on by the art connoisseurs, who didn't regard it as 'proper' art. It was the new freedom to paint what they wanted that led lots of painters at the time to choose this subject matter and make it popular. Travel, also, was becoming much easier, with the railways spreading their tentacles throughout a Britain on the verge of an industrial revolution.

But maybe the huge changes still wouldn't have happened at all if two remarkable landscape painters, as different as chalk and cheese, hadn't started exhibiting their wares on the London art scene.

JOHN CONSTABLE (1776–1837)

John Constable *Flatford Mill* 1816–17

It's difficult to dispute the fact that if you've got a rich dad (and a bit of talent) it's much easier to forge ahead in the fine arts. There's none of that old having-to-make-a-living business to get in the way of creativity. John Constable was no exception, being the son of a wealthy Suffolk mill owner who went to the Royal Academy in 1799 and didn't flog as much as a doodle for twelve years after leaving. His work was eventually regarded as a breath of fresh air after the limp but pretty Romantic styles of chaps like Gainsborough and Claude Lorrain. Constable's paintings looked more like the work of some of the nearly forgotten mid-seventeenth-century Dutch painters.

All Constable wanted to do was show his beloved countryside as it really was, instead of using all the slick tricks of the more fashionable painters of the time. He'd go out and draw nature, until he had enough to come home and elaborate on the sketches. Many people, myself included, believe he could have saved himself a whole load of time and trouble, by sticking with these oil sketches which were truly masterful. It could be said that his finished paintings lack the same vitality, often appearing to be rather over-worked. Say that amongst a group of Constable fans, however, and you could have your tongue ripped out.

Constable hit stardom when he exhibited a painting called *The Haywain* in Paris in 1824. It is a painting that no one can ever avoid, as it's been reproduced on absolutely everything from table mats to greetings cards to tea towels to God-knows-what-else. It's very easy, however, to take the mickey out of something because of its immense popularity. After all, the general public is so often a fool. In a recent survey among ordinary British people, the most popular, and most heard of painter was, wait for it, Rolf (tie me kangaroo down, sport') Harris. My case rests. But, even bearing this in mind, there is still a certain slightly sleazy idealism about the way Mr Constable sees the countryside that seems to make it a distant cousin of all the junk you see in seaside art galleries, on the railings at Hyde Park, or printed on those horrid, naff plates advertised in the back of colour supplements.

JOSEPH MALLORD WILLIAM TURNER (1775–1851)

If you're into Constable then there's a fair chance you won't want a Turner over the fireplace. Turner wasn't interested in charming little scenes from country life: deliciously picturesque poor people going about their everyday drudgery with daft smiles on their ruddy (but honest) faces. He preferred to illustrate, in his own way, the magnificence and sheer power of nature – painting with great gusto and pulling every trick out of the book to achieve what had hitherto been regarded as impossible. You might think his stuff pretentious, overworked and ill-defined, but I get the impression that if Turner was around to hear you say it, he would give a popular two-finger sign and simply carry on regardless.

J. M. W. Turner *Peace – Burial at Sea* 1841

He painted the countryside and the sea in all its moods, weather-wise, from blissful serenity to extreme turbulence. It is said that on one occasion the silly ass actually had himself tied to the wheel of a ship to witness, at first hand, the power of the wind and the sea during a storm. I've heard of suffering for your art, but, Bill – that is plain stupid!

Don't seek out a Turner if you want your Is dotted or your Ts crossed detail-wise. He had no time or need for all that stuff and, rather like Guardi the Venetian master a hundred years earlier, would use a couple of deft brushstrokes to imply what could take someone else hours to put in (to no greater effect).

There is little doubt that this method of work anticipated all those French Impressionists by many years, and in Turner's own final years he even showed leanings towards a kind of Abstract Expressionism (*see* p. 160).

Other Great Eighteenth-century Painters' Names to Drop

John Singleton Copley and Benjamin West (American), Caspar David Friedrich (German), Jean-Antoine Houdon (French).

CHAPTER 21

Renaissance Time Again

Art in the Nineteenth Century

While the French had been revolting in the early eighteenth century (no jokes please!), circumstances began to change for your everyday artist in Britain and they were beginning to suffer the onslaught of the Industrial Revolution. Humble workshops were growing into factories and newfangled machines were churning out artefacts by the million.

In architecture, the changes were even more obvious. Buildings were shooting up all over England and America and the term 'built-up area' was becoming common. Style-wise architecture was like a ship that had broken from its anchor. The main bits of the buildings were fairly plain, boring and functional . . . but then the poor architect was ordered to stick on an arty façade to make it either Gothic, Norman, Renaissance or even oriental. Churches were usually Gothic; music halls Baroque or Rococo; while palaces and posh houses were more often in the Italian High Renaissance style. As you can imagine, buildings started to look like a dog's breakfast and the successful architect was the one who didn't think too much about compromise when trying to make a few bob.

So they had all these trashy, cheap, machine-made goods produced to decorate the middle-class home, pouring on to the market. Horrid ornaments, bad pottery and cheap sentimental prints became the hallmark of the new middle-class living room.

'Proper' artists began to be regarded with deep suspicion by 'respectable' people with regular jobs. How dare they charge such huge amounts for something so inconsequential and overrated? The artists soon began to react to this and deliberately went out to play to the gallery and shock the pants off the population at large. They grew beards (the men, that is), wore scruffy corduroy workers' clothes, grew their hair long, drank too much, loosened their morals and were regarded by your man in the street as the punks were in 1970s England. (It's nice to know nothing's changed.)

Unfortunately, like all movements that ever tried to be eccentric, the individualism that the artist had been craving soon got lost. After a while, they all began to look and sound the same. Thankfully, expressing oneself artistically has never had anything to do with how one looks (Elton John please note!).

Serious art lovers had a slightly different angle. Because art had lost most of its other functions it now existed purely to express personality. To those who cared about art, technical skill was no longer the biggest deal – you could see it anywhere. Moreover, this tiny percentage of the enlightened public wanted to mix and speak with these new men of integrity and incorruptible sincerity – pure artists who wouldn't make even the tiniest mark on a piece of canvas unless it was for the very best of reasons.

The history of art had therefore turned a fairly large corner. Maybe the perceived masters, albeit extremely skilful, were still getting all the best commissions, the best loot and therefore the best fame, but now an ever-growing group of young artists was daring to shun 'official art' and paint purely for its own satisfaction.

Unfortunately we only usually get to hear of people like this when they're six feet under but history, bless it, now tends to remember these previously unsung heroes, rather than the fat cats who knocked out all the boring statues of famous men in town squares, murals and windows for grand palaces, and the decorations for town halls and municipal buildings. At last art history had taken note of this group of often lonely, always passionate and mostly misunderstood guys instead of what had until now been a bit of a *Who's Who* of wealthy artists.

Paris Painters

If Florence had been the place to be in the fifteenth century and Rome in the seventeenth, Paris was becoming most definitely where it was at in the nineteenth. Artists and would-be artists flocked from all over the world to dress up in daft outfits and sit around in cafés drinking cheap wine and talking pretentiously about where art was going.

JEAN-AUGUSTE-DOMINIQUE INGRES (1780–1867)

Ingres was the most famous of the 'straight', classical artists of the time. An ex-student of David (of Marat-in-the-bath fame), he despised anything that even looked like an expression of free thought. His stuff hit the pinnacle of form and finish but this very perfection, and often absurdly sentimental imagery, made him hated amongst the new wave of artists searching for something a bit more substantial. Though no doubt a genius with the old brushes and paint, I personally think that many of his famous paintings of nude women are so flawless and wrinkle free that they look a bit like heavily retouched centre spreads in *Playboy* (so I've heard).

Jean-Auguste-Dominique Ingres *Venus Anadyomene* 1848

EUGÈNE DELACROIX (1798–1863)

Eugene Delacroix *Greece Expiring on the ruins of Missolonghi* 1827

These angry young painter-persons found a voice, or should I say canvas, in one Eugène Delacroix. Delacroix was a right rebel and even a bit of a revolutionary but only, I should add, in art. For a start, he loathed the academics (all that bull about the classical splendour of Greeks and Romans). While Ingres and his followers preferred Poussin and the Grand Manner, Delacroix and his lads were into the vibrancy of Rubens and the wild Venetians (no prizes for guessing where my sympathies lie).

Delacroix was far more interested in colour as opposed to draughtsmanship and was prepared to sacrifice knowledge for imagination. He found he couldn't even bear to look at the subject matter chosen by Ingres and the academics and eventually hightailed it off to North Africa where he produced loads of wonderful, passionate pictures of frightfully bloodthirsty battles with all the vigour and colour of the Arab world.

Le Réalisme

Back in mid-century France, also reacting against the academic style, a group of painters, who'd been totally blown away by the work of our boy Constable, set up in a little village called Barbizon in order to record rural life at first hand. The poor peasants must have got really hacked off with these blasted artists popping out from behind the hedgerows every five minutes to draw them while they were trying to do an honest day's work. The results, when their canvases were sent back to the highly sophisticated Paris, were regarded as revolutionary, as peasants had always been regarded as a bit of a joke. The Réalisme movement is therefore defined as 'a Romantic quest to find beauty in the bizarre or the conventionally ugly' which I think sounds like a real cheek.

GUSTAVE COURBET (1819–77)

Courbet spearheaded this group of élitist voyeurs and had a one-man show in a little shack in Paris in 1855. Mind you, that doesn't mean much. These days even a Parisian shack would cost a jambe et un bras. To be fair to Courbet and co., they didn't do it just for the francs; they really wanted to shock the art world by showing it a subject matter that had never even been considered before.

Courbet himself cared only about truth to nature, much as the late, great Caravaggio had done years before. In his rather funny painting *Bonjour Monsieur Courbet* Gustave can be recognized as a rather weird-looking backpacker with arguably the daftest beard ever seen, meeting a couple of guys on a country path. Its awkward composition and total lack of any academic conventions was deliberately painted to shock the art establishment. Funny really, these days you have to cast your own head in blood (*see* Marc Quinn p. 190) to get the same reaction. The French bourgeoisie didn't want their artists or their art to look like that, which pleased Courbet no end. This new concept of painting for oneself, as opposed to what the art market demanded, caught on like wildfire with many of the young painters and sculptors hanging around the Paris scene.

Gustav Courbet *Bonjour Monsieur Courbet* 1854

Courbet wasn't remembered for his modesty, however. When asked what style of painting he followed, the cocky so-and-so replied, 'I am a Courbetist. My painting is the only true one. I am the first and only artist of this century. The others are students and drivellers.' Cor blimey, Courbet! I don't somehow think you'll find too many experts to agree with you.

Other Great Early Nineteenth-century Painters' Names to Drop

Jean-François Millet, Jean-Baptiste Carpeaux (sculptor), Antoine Gros, Théodore Géricault, Honoré Daumier, Rosa Bonheur.

CHAPTER 22

Back for the Future

Pre-Raphaelite Brotherhood

Sir Edward Burne-Jones
The Golden Stairs 1880

It is now established that the academics were hellbent on following the Grand Manner and the style of old Raphael, who was head of the idealizing nature school. In 1848, while revolutions were all the rage throughout Europe, a small group of Englishmen got together to try to get art out of that particular rut and recapture 'the directness and simplicity of painting before Raphael' (a bit like trying to reinvent the wheel!).

The main, or should I say most famous, Brothers were William Holman Hunt, Dante Gabriel Rossetti, John Everett Millais and Ford Maddox Brown, who, though never a fully paid-up member, has always been associated with them.

It was a terribly arty, and not a little pompous, gang, who had the nerve to draw up a 'List of Immortals' which consisted exclusively of – three guesses – artists and writers. Their aim was to restore art 'to a moral seriousness' which they thought was so lacking in 'stale academic art' (and to make a few quid, I'll be bound). Many people think they achieved the very opposite, creating a series of pretentious canvases that had about as much meaning as a day in Disneyland.

The subject matter was literary, religious and always very sentimental. In fact, I now realize that the few attendance stamps I got as a kid at Sunday school were tiny reproductions of their work. For me they define the difference between painting and illustration. Despite the fact that they imitated the technique of the great fresco artists like Raphael or Tiepolo, working in bright (sometimes garish) colours on a wet white background, their paintings lack depth, truth or any lasting emotional content. The only thing that really differentiates them from illustrations is that they're big.

A typical example of the stuff they turned out would be the *Knight Errant* by Millais, in which one can see a rather kind knight who has just happened to stumble across a beautiful, blonde-haired maiden tied to a tree with not even a stray leaf to cover her nakedness (things like that never happen to me!). We are tempted to ask what a knight in full armour was doing in the woods in the first place – which leads me further to wonder whether he really was, in fact, *un*tying the poor girl as we are led to suppose. For all we know he might have been doing the very opposite – you know what knights were like!

It might sound from all this that I don't go for the Pre-Raphaelites. On the contrary I think they're fab and even have some (reproductions) hanging in the loo (as opposed to the Louvre). There's nothing the matter with a good old-fashioned piece of kitsch. They also have a strange and almost sinister perfection about them, with all the human subjects looking like they've been chosen from a 70s model catalogue – like beautiful half-dead and totally stoned flower people. To me the Pre-Raphaelites are to painting what junk food is to proper food. Delicious and easy to consume but, in the end, of little nutritional value.

Other Great Pre-Raphaelites' Names to Drop

Thomas Woolner, James Collinson, Sir Edward Burne-Jones.

CHAPTER 23

Backwards or Forwards?

Art Nouveau

Towards the end of the nineteenth century, Western Europe was showing signs of across-the-board prosperity. Artists, although perfectly prepared to make money out of such situations, are notorious for rebelling and missing the boat. This period was no exception. Strangely enough it was buildings that became the main target. Just about everything that went up still looked as if it had come from a pattern book of historical styles, with columns, cornices, mouldings, you name it, tacked on wherever there wasn't a window. Even Joe Public was getting restless. He was fed up with the machine-made, soulless, uniform ornamentations and craved for the craftsmen of the past.

John Ruskin and William Morris (of wallpaper fame) put their aesthetic feet down and rather naïvely – especially following an industrial revolution – demanded that artists and sculptors should return to medieval conditions. Most artists thought this a load of cobblers and instead demanded and searched for a new art.

It started properly in 1890 when a few architects began in earnest to look around for new designs and new materials. Why, they said, shouldn't the new building materials like iron and glass have a decorative style of their own?

They looked eastwards, particularly to the Chinese and Japanese, with their swirly plant forms and stylized imagery from nature. Whistler (*see* Whistler, p. 119) had been telling everyone to look in that direction for years but no one had listened.

AUBREY BEARDSLEY (1872–98)

In drawing, it was a young, rather limp-wristed, British illustrator called Aubrey Beardsley who hit the headlines throughout Europe with his starkly simple (and often really rude), Japanese-influenced black and white drawings.

It is interesting to note that there was a huge revival of his style in the late 1960s and 70s when the pot-smoking, underground hippie movement embraced it (and thought it original). In Paris the famous French small-person Henri de Toulouse-Lautrec, while waiting for Post Impressionism to be invented, busied himself producing wonderfully strong and atmospheric posters in the Art Nouveau style.

Aubrey Beardsley *Salome* 1892

As a postscript, Art Nouveau was only really a fashion or style that ended as soon as it began, rather than a true art movement. Having said that, ornaments and artefacts in this style are still much sought after by the rich and trendy.

Other Art Nouveau Names to Drop

Victor Hortha, Louis Tiffany, Hippolyte Lucus, Gustuv Klimt, Sir Frank Brangwyn.

CHAPTER 24

Impressionism

1860s

You have go to a long way to find someone who doesn't think the Impressionists were fab. Let's face it, we have enough chances to see their work. Practically every range of calendars, chocolate boxes or naff greeting cards will have used Impressionist paintings at some time or other.

The movement really hit the headlines when Édouard Manet and his mate Claude Monet (I bet you thought they were one and the same) became the first to paint what they thought they saw rather than what they actually saw. You see?

Up to that time most of the wimpish classical painters, obviously sensitive to the cold and damp, scurried back to their nice, warm studios with their sketches to finish them off. The trouble was that they painted their landscapes using the same methods as they'd used for their still lifes: that is, using one source of light (usually from the window). This tended to make their vision of the world a touch boring, with everything in its 'correct' place and in its proper colour, a bit like those awful model landscapes that some weird men run their awful model trains through.

All Change

The Impressionists reckoned that nature didn't actually work like that and kicked out this formal use of colour and 'tidied-up' placing of objects in a landscape. Legoland was definitely not their cup of *thé*. Instead they believed that nature never stood still and that the objects in a landscape were made up of trillions of colours that reacted to whatever light was thrown upon them. All the artist was required to do was soak up this information, allowing it to swill around under his beret, until an impression of what he'd just been looking at would pour on to the canvas. That was the theory anyway.

Not Impressed

And they certainly made some sort of an impression. They caused a stir that even Madonna's mum would have been proud of. The art critics of the time went barmy – 'lunatic daubings by extravagant heretics' was how one of the more moderate ones put it.

But they were soon to eat their words, however, for as the stream of sketchy, unrefined, brightly coloured canvases streamed into Gay Paree from the surrounding countryside, the art-buying public, fed up with being told what it should and shouldn't like, decided after some time to show *deux doigts* to the critics, put their hands deep into their pockets, and invest their hard-earned francs. Some of the lads, like Monet and Renoir, became not only *très célèbre* but, more to the point, *très riche*! Had those crabby critics hedged their bets when it all started, and bought the odd picture cheap, they'd have really cleaned up. As it was, formal art criticism was to take a kick from which it never really recovered. Those brave Impressionists will always be a shining example to all those painters forever bashing their heads against the Establishment. It could almost be said that they did for art what Pavarotti did for opera (and fat people!).

So let's look a little closer at these men who have captured the imaginations of people who otherwise wouldn't give a fig for art.

EDOUARD MANET (1832–83)

Édouard Manet *Déjeuner sur l'Herbe* 1863

Manet and his chums, although not exactly fans of Courbet, did agree with his rejection of academic painting, which they too thought had become as stale as old French loaves. To us, however, his early paintings might not look that different. OK, the contrasts of colour, light and shade were a bit more exaggerated, and the finish not all it might be, but not enough to cause the outcry that came from all the 'straight' artists of mid-nineteenth-century Paris. It was Manet and his mates who caused the now notorious 'Salon of the Rejected' to be put on in 1863 as a snub to the outraged jury of the proper Salon (the name of the exhibition) to which their work had originally been submitted. The jury thought, quite rightly as it happened, that it would give the Parisian public a good laugh.

Manet was gobsmacked. He didn't want to be a revolutionary. After all, he thought the much-talked-about Pre-Raphaelites were crap and looked for inspiration in the work of late greats like Giorgione, Titian and Velázquez.

The trouble was, the general public at first thought, as many viewers of modern art still do now, that detail means realism; or that if a painter leaves something out of a painting, like the features of a face or the fingers of a hand, it is because he either can't actually do them, or he simply can't be bothered. What they fail to realize is that very often by leaving such details out of a picture, or by purely using blocks of flat colour, an effect can be reached that is more realistic than all the detail in the world.

CLAUDE MONET (1840–1926)

Claude Monet *The Beach at Trouville* 1870

Manet's mate Monet, although a bit of a misery, was uncompromising in his approach to painting. He flatly refused to do a single brushstroke indoors. If the subject wasn't in front of him from start to finish he wasn't interested. He even had a little boat fitted out like a studio so that he could stay on the river for as long as possible. Like his two friends Pissarro and Sisley, he didn't bother with all that mixing of thin subtle colour washes, sensitively applied over dark brown foundations as the oldtimers had done. No, they preferred to slosh the paint straight on to the canvas using brilliant intense strokes, to catch the atmosphere and visual mood before it passed.

This, as we know, drove their critics, who seriously thought they were simply taking the Piss-arro, to near hysteria. But if Impressionism could have had a core, Monet would have to be it. Even the name Impressionism had come from his highly ridiculed painting *Impression, Sunrise.* Funny really, of London's National Gallery's list of the most popular paintings of all time, based on postcard sales, Monet's *Water Lilies* came out top.

He was obsessed, even more than the others, with light and how it changes and influences everything it plays on. Sometimes when you close your eyes in front of a brilliant scene, the image stays as if printed on the inside of your eyelids. Monet's paintings are a bit like that; their brilliance and sparkle almost jump from the canvas.

AUGUSTE RENOIR (1841–1919)

This chum of Monet's was unashamedly fond of painting pretty young girls with not many clothes on and gay Parisians having a good time (seems fine to me). His work often had even less detail than the other Impressionists and consequently attracted more flak from the baying art critics. They just couldn't get it into their silly French heads that very often putting every single detail into a picture stands a fair chance of rendering it dull, flat and lifeless. Just as Leonardo had used *sfumato* to hide a multitude of detail in his dark shadows, Renoir used patches of colour. The Impressionists were the first to realize that you couldn't really get away with Leonardo's trick when painting outside, especially in sunlight. They recognized that the human eye is dead clever, only needing a hint of something it has seen before in order to communicate the rest to the brain, much as Guardi had done with his figures in a Venetian landscape.

Pierre-Auguste Renoir *The Umbrellas c.*1880–85

It wasn't the artists' fault that the Paris critics looked at their pictures with their noses only inches from the canvas making them all look like an unrelated jumble of shapes and colours. Talk about not seeing the wood for the trees! At that distance they couldn't see the wood *or* the trees.

EDGAR DEGAS (1834–1917)

Degas, like Manet, didn't like to be associated too closely with the rest of the Impressionist gang. Bad for sales, I suppose. He actually thought himself rather above it all and confessed to being a fan of Ingres (someone had to be).

His most famous paintings and pastel drawings were of nubile ballet dancers and racehorses; not, he claimed, because he liked or fancied them (the dancers), but more because he was able to regard them with the same dispassionate objectiveness as the other Impressionists treated landscapes (if you can believe that, you can believe anything).

Degas reckoned he was alone in tackling a whole set of new problems: like how light interacts with the human form, and how to suggest space and movement in a manner that the whole academic world hadn't even thought of. In order to do this, he maintained, he had to be a master of design. Do I detect a little insecurity and self-justification there, Edgar?

Edgar Degas *Cotton Exchange in New Orleans* 1873

AUGUSTE RODIN (1840–1917)

It wasn't only in paint that the Impressionists found their 'voice'. The great French sculptor Rodin, though not really regarded as a club member was up to his neck in the battle for or against modernism. To be absolutely fair, Rodin didn't have the same argument with classical art and worshipped the guvnors – Leonardo and Michelangelo.

Unlike many of his contemporaries, he made a fortune and became *très* famous well within his own lifetime, being deeply admired by the general public.

Auguste Rodin *The Kiss* c.1901–4

The reason Rodin is put on the Impressionists' side is quite simple. He, like them, saw absolutely no point in finish for its own sake, preferring, like them, to leave as much as possible to the imagination. Many of his sculptures, in fact, appeared to grow naturally out of a rough old lump of rock. This was like a gesture of defiance to his critics who accused him of laziness. Like Rembrandt he claimed that a piece was finished when he'd done what he'd set out to do – so there! The bits that Rodin did finish were nothing short of brilliant and he showed off the skill factor that the punters craved. His association and sympathy with those dreadful, scruffy Impressionists, therefore, did them nothing but good.

Other Great Impressionists' Names to Drop

Camille Pissarro, Alfred Sisley, Berthe Morisot.

CHAPTER 25

France Impresses England

Impressionism at Home

The fame of the Impressionists soon hit England through contemporary painters like James Abbott McNeill Whistler (1834–1903) who, as you might have guessed from his name, was an American by birth. He decided, after exhibiting with Manet at the now famous 'Salon of the Rejected' in Paris, to cross the Channel to be rejected in London.

Despite his often subtle and evocative paintings, Whistler was a right troublemaker and once confessed to a hobby of 'making enemies'. Unlike the large group of Impressionists who were having a ball fighting for recognition in Paris, poor Whistler had to fight for 'modern art' alone in London. His greatest foe was the horrendously influential critic John Ruskin who, despite supporting the decidedly lightweight Pre-Raphaelites, thought Whistler a load of rubbish and told everyone so.

James Abbott-McNeil Whistler *Nocturne in Blue and Gold (old Battersea Bridge)* *c.*1872

Ruskin eventually went well over the top and Whistler sued him for accusing him of flinging the paint at the canvas and charging a fortune for, at the most, a couple of days' work. Whistler won the case by stating that his public paid not for the amount of time spent on each picture, but for the knowledge of a lifetime that went into those two days' work. Up yours, Ruskin!

This case may now be regarded as a watershed artwise, as it neatly separated 'modern art' from everything that had gone before. Up to this time, with few exceptions, art had been valued at how much hard work you got for your cash. It was easy to see why the punters would part with pocketfuls for the work of, say, Canaletto, Rubens or even the often laboured Pre-Raphaelites. They could see exactly how much meticulous effort had gone into their paintings; but when painters like Whistler offered another angle to the value of a work of art, the 'Get Home Early' school of painting was ready to be born.

At last, it wasn't how much paint was put on the canvas, but what that paint actually meant that counted. Mind you, I suspect that if poor Whistler had realized that his statement was to eventually lead to modern painters like Mark Rothko (*see* Mark Rothko, p. 163) or Jackson (king of paint-throwing) Pollock, he'd probably have thought twice. Once you leave the 'value for money' or 'is it very well drawn' methods of evaluating art you get on to very dodgy and constantly shifting ground. The uneducated (whatever that means) man in the street falls instant prey to the critics and dealers who always have the last say on what's good and what isn't.

Here comes the Emperor with or without new clothes. Read on!

CHAPTER 26

Proper Modern Art

Post Impressionism

Impressionism became well established and it looked like it would be around for years. But as soon as artists become happy with a style, they start casting around for something new. Impressionism was fine as far as it went but it didn't seem to be proper 'modern art'. It was still only trying to reproduce nature as it really was, and the Impressionists' quarrel, if you want to call it that, with the academics was only about the best way of going about it. The Impressionists had more or less cracked it, but that implied that all art was now about was showing things as they really looked. Let's face it, the newfangled photography was coming along fast and so art would soon be required to come up with other ways of viewing reality. Even some of the artists who'd been in the forefront of the Impressionist movement refused to believe that it was the final station at the end of the painting line.

PAUL CÉZANNE (1839–1906)

Cézanne had been quite happy being an Impressionist, but was becoming fed up with having all the critics continually snapping at his heels. Luckily he was never strapped for cash, having had a rich daddy, so after the arty, boozy life of Paris he caught the train home to Aix where he reckoned he could lead a much more peaceful and productive country life. After all, he thought, who wants to waste time talking about painting if it takes you away from actually doing it?

He didn't mind his Impressionist chums, but thought their work messy and unstructured. We now know he was fiddling around with concepts of Cubism, but even *he* didn't know that, as

Paul Cézanne *The Card Players* c.1892–95

it hadn't been invented yet. Poor Cézanne never really felt he achieved what he was looking for, but art history and the stupendous prices his paintings now fetch, tend to disagree. He is now regarded as perhaps one of the finest painters of the modern movement. Many think that Cézanne invented it.

But is it Modern Art?

It is in his still lifes that we see how radical and new Cézanne's approach was. Unlike the old Dutch masters who simply used the still life to show off how damn clever they were technically, Cézanne pushed and shoved, squeezed and stretched all the objects in his compositions, regardless of accuracy, to achieve a true and balanced harmony. He thought nothing of mucking around with perspective, shadows and even proportions to get what he wanted. He 'bullied' his landscapes in the same way, but as we don't always know the scene that he was actually painting we can't realize just how much he pulled it about.

Despite all this, the famous art historian Venturi said of Cézanne: 'There is nothing decadent, nothing abstract, no art for art's sake in his character and work; nothing but an innate and indomitable will to create art.'

GEORGES SEURAT (1859–91)

Georges Seurat *The Bathers* 1883

If you've ever seen the cards that opticians use to test for colour blindness, or early computer printouts of pictures, you'll have some idea what a Seurat ('sewer rat' to you) painting looks like. Not that he was colour blind; in fact the very opposite. He built up tiny dots of pure colour like a mosaic to achieve an overall effect that could only be understood from a few feet back (he used a really long paintbrush). Seurat had studied optics and colour and was obsessed by the division of light into its constituent colours. The result was that his outdoor scenes actually shimmer with an almost uncanny brilliance. The technique became known as Pointillism.

Poor Seurat died young, but his influence was enormous on

such all-time greats as Picasso and Braque and the Italian Futurist movement. The combination of his early demise and the ridiculously laborious way of covering the canvas means there are unfortunately very few of his pictures around.

Vincent Van Gogh *Wheat Fields and Cypress Trees* 1889

While young Seurat was gaining a reputation in Paris, a young Dutch vicar's son called Vincent Van Gogh left Paris in search of the sunshine, sanity and brilliant light of the south. He was financed by his younger brother and, although he thought one day he'd be able to pay him back, died francless (and earless). Ironic really, if he'd been alive today he could have practically bought France on the strength of just a few paintings.

After a year of the southern life he went almost totally bonkers but, surprisingly, managed to hold together enough to paint some of his very finest landscapes. It all seems rather odd: here was a man with an incredible talent, protected from the horrible world of bills, living in one of the most beautiful locations, regularly visiting Paris for all the café life and pretty *jeunes filles* he could handle, and yet still he couldn't hack it. At thirty-seven he topped himself, depriving the art world of maybe hundreds of canvases.

Mind you, it must be said that if you look a bit closer at a Van Gogh of this later period, you can sense his state of mind by the slightly frenzied use of the brush. Like Cézanne, he wasn't the least bit interested in painting a 'portrait' of a landscape; he just wanted his audience to *feel* what it was actually like to be there. Both Van Gogh and Cézanne worked neither to please nor upset their critics, they just painted because they had to. The later work of Van Gogh was to lead directly to the Expressionist movement (which is coming soon).

Unlike Cézanne, Van Gogh never really wanted to work alone and dreamed of a brotherhood of like-minded artists, a bit like the Pre-Raphaelites (heaven forbid), but, unfortunately, he was such a fruitcake that nobody could stand him for very long. One who lasted longer than most was a young successful stockbroker-cum-weekend-painter whom he'd met in Paris and worked with in the country...

PAUL GAUGUIN (1848–1903)

A very strange and complex man who failed to make it as a painter in France and couldn't support his wife and family after the comparative riches of a 'proper job'. He was, sad to say, always too timid as a person for the strength of the statements he was trying to make. Until, that is, he packed his paints and escaped to the southern seas – Tahiti to be precise – to produce the stunningly atmospheric paintings that were to make him a cornerstone of modern art. OK, most of his subjects were rather grumpy natives lying about in grass huts, but his use of colour and composition was so completely new and off the wall that he became almost a school of painting in his own right.

With Gauguin the subject matter was very much what it was all about, insomuch as he could not express himself properly until

Paul Gaugin *The Spirit of the Dead Watching* 1892

he found an exotic enough subject. He must, unfortunately, have done more than just paint the natives as he died aged fifty-five of chronic syphilis.

These poor, unhappy chappies started down the four roads leading to what we now call modern art.

Cézanne's slightly fragmented order was to lead to Cubism.

Seurat's breaking of light into its constituent parts was picked up by the Futurists.

Van Gogh's need to feel a subject as well as look at it, led to Expressionism.

Gauguin's simple, back-to-basics quest was to lead to the revitalization of Primitivism.

HENRI DE TOULOUSE-LAUTREC (1864–1901)

Both Gauguin and Van Gogh had at some stage become well underwhelmed by the spiritual state of the Western World, to the

Henri de Toulouse-Lautrec
Tête-à-Tête Supper 1899

point of obsession. One man who lived and worked in Paris positively thrived on it and thought decadence to be enormous fun. Henri de Toulouse-Lautrec was certainly behind *la porte* when looks were given out. Not only was he a dwarf, but an extremely ugly one at that. He spent all his time in nightclubs and brothels and his models were the dancers, prostitutes and pimps who were his best mates. His drawings and paintings had a vitality hitherto unseen, especially when one considers the 'outrageous' subject matter. He did not glorify or patronize his surroundings, however, and was certainly not to be linked to the other rather prettifying, 'slice of life' Impressionists. Henri portrayed the seamy side of life with total truth and lashings of love, showing all the ugliness and falseness of a Paris at the height of its decadence.

In fact, far from trying to tart the ugly side up (if you'll pardon the expression), Toulouse-Lautrec loved that bit best. If you're going to be a pervert, be a real pervert. The poor little genius died an alcoholic at the age of thirty-seven.

Other Great Names

There weren't any!

CHAPTER 27

Where To Now?

Twentieth-century Art

A brand-new century, and time to take stock of what was going on in the world of art. It was, sadly, all looking a little tired; not because of the art itself, but more because of the artists – who were all getting a bit long in the tooth. In fact, many of the great painters were, metaphorically speaking, squeezing the last dollop out of their tubes.

Gauguin, for instance, had just set off on his third escape from his family and finances to the south seas where he was to get well miserable, catch the clap and promptly die; Van Gogh and Seurat had already hung up their berets and ascended to the big painting in the sky; Toulouse-Lautrec had peered longingly up his very last can-can girl's skirt, and was being measured for a very short coffin; Monet was still going strong but was beginning to go blind (a bit of a drag in the painting game); and Renoir, although soon to be a still life, was still managing to churn out some fab paintings.

Despite all this, Paris was still the Mecca for artists and acted as a magnet to anyone who wanted to jump on the bandwagon (or recently invented aeroplane) or start a movement of his own. At this time there were so many 'isms' around that a few new ones would hardly have been noticed. There was Impressionism, Post Impressionism, Romanticism, Pointillism, Neo-Classicism, Realism, You-name-it-ism, all rattling around in one city.

Anyone who wanted to earn (or paint) his stripes as an artist simply had to be seen there at some time or other. Perhaps the only other place that attracted artists was the German city of Munich; not particularly for the visual aspect of art that was there, but for the academic and intellectual reputation of the city. Soon-to-be-rated artists like Paul Klee and Wassily Kandinsky not only struggled to make the right marks on canvas but also, and much more important (to them), to find out what the marks meant and why they were making 'em.

Primitivism

Gauguin had discovered Primitivism and in some ways this was going to have a bigger effect on 'modern art' than both Expressionism and Cubism put together. It was in the year of the Fauves (*see* Fauves, p. 134) that a huge interest in early medieval art, and the stuff turned out by naïve natives in far continents, began to rival that of the academicians who seemed only to be able to worship (or grovel) at the feet of Greek sculpture.

An amateur artist from the Parisian suburbs began to be talked about throughout the cafés of Paris amongst Picasso and his mates, even if it was only to take the mickey.

HENRI ROUSSEAU (1844–1910)

Henri Rousseau *The Dream* 1910

A weekend painter who'd had no training whatsoever and had just retired from being a customs collector, Henri Rousseau had no clue as to how to draw properly, and knew little about Impressionism. Here was a self-taught star who painted with simple, pure colours and strong not-to-be-confused outlines. The joke was, his hero was Ingres, whom all his other Impressionist fans loathed. We can thank God that he never got the hang of 'proper' painting. Unlike the Impressionists, Rousseau never knew what to leave out, so he left everything in – right down to the last leaf on the last tree. Picasso paid five francs for an early Rousseau, which was quite a good deal seeing as his work was to become incredibly valuable (not that Picasso needed the cash). His painting has been copied right up to this day, particularly among current illustrators. If there's one thing I hate, however, it's forced naïvety. It's like learning how to build a car complete with engine, and then having it pulled by a horse.

Many would have it that Rousseau was the true father of modern art. The jury's still out.

CHAPTER 28

STOP PRESS !!!

Owing to the modern art world taking itself so ridiculously seriously (and silly copyright laws) there can be no further reproductions.

Cubism

or How to See the Back of Something from the Front

Mention the term 'modern art' to someone who only buys his wall decorations from Woolworth's or car-boot sales, and he'll rearrange himself nervously and make some glib comment like, 'I wouldn't give it house room,' or 'You can only tell which way up it goes by looking for the hook on the back.' Nine times out of ten our layperson will have Pablo Picasso in the back of his mind, and more than likely, his Cubist period.

PABLO AND GEORGES

Although most art critics seem to agree that Cubism was invented by Pablo Picasso (1881–1973) with not a little help from his chum Georges Braque (1882–1963), it now seems fair to suggest that it might have been all Cézanne's fault. It appears that he casually mentioned to one of his students that her compositions would be helped if she looked upon nature as a series of cones, cylinders and spheres (much as Walt Disney advised animators years later). Pablo and Georges, being the sharp young Parisians they no doubt were, took old Cézanne's words a bit too literally and, never ones to miss a new trend, commenced to turn everything in front of them into a series of geometric patterns and cubes, much to the growing dismay of their growing gaggle of arty groupies.

And they didn't stop there! Not content with jumbling up their subjects from one angle (face on), they started mixing up this view with loads of other angles. Just to pile on the confusion, they began painting the backgrounds the same colour and tone as the stuff in the foreground, whose outer edges they broke up. By the time the paint was dry, one would have been hard put to work out what the darn thing was of! The two young artists thought this all thrilling stuff and claimed they'd solved the eternal puzzle of painting – that is, how to show real depth when working on a flat surface.

Crabby Critics

Those old critics didn't see it that way, needless to say, and thought it a rotten cheek to expect the viewer to hunt around the picture for the odd ear, foot or nipple in order to unearth a nude, or unscramble a jumble of random bottles and bits of old French cheese to discover a still life.

The Cubists (by this time a growing bunch) did, however, realize the dodgy ground they were treading, so kept their subject matter mostly to the aforementioned dismembered women or simple household objects. Eventually (as always), the critics came round when they realized there was cash in all this confusion, and hailed Picasso as a genius yet again. Pablo simply pocketed the cash and went on to look for pastures new, though it must be said that he never really managed to leave these Cubist roots.

Many people, like myself, have always been a bit suspicious of Cubism. Is it really a worthwhile contribution to the development of twentieth-century painting, or just a swish technique that, once you got the hang of it, was fairly easy to churn out? I find Picasso's 'portrait' of Ambroise Vollard, for instance, deeply dodgy. At first glance you see your run-of-the-mill, back-to-front Cubist painting. In the middle of this, standing out like a rhino at a penguins' party, is the floating head of, we must presume, Monsieur Vollard.

This head obviously hasn't been given the full treatment or we (or more to the point M. Vollard) wouldn't be able to see who the heck the portrait was of. Therefore our Pablo has given it a bit of light Cubism, which begs the question: is Cubism just an intellectual hide and seek or just a quaint affectation like Pre-Raphaelitism and Art Nouveau?

CHAPTER 29

Art Goes Wild!

The Fauves

In Paris, between 1905 and 1907, the trendy young painters thought that Impressionism was a bit sissy, but were generally still into guys like Van Gogh and Cézanne, who had rejected naturalistic forms and colour. The Fauves took it much further, going into bold, often garish, colours and gross distortion. They bunched together and were nicknamed the 'Fauves' (Wild Beasts), an insult of which they rather approved. I must admit that I still find it hard to tell the difference between them and the soon-to-be-mentioned Expressionists, especially in the early stages.

HENRI MATISSE (1869–1954)

Henri Matisse, an ex-lawyer, was the leader and founder of the Fauves. His pet hate had been painters like Seurat, whom he thought was just a technician. He claimed Seurat treated everything in the same way leaving nothing, in the end, but an insignificant, gimmicky effect – much like the French singers of the time, who had started putting that dreadful Edith Piaf-type wobble in their voices.

Matisse not only went on about what he didn't like, but on and on about what he did. To be fair, who's ever heard of a lawyer (albeit ex) who could say something in a few words when a thousand would do?

Matisse himself had, and still has to this day, an immense following amongst designers and colourists who regard him as their all-time guru. The slightest criticism often sends his fans wild. His early work often reminds one of kids' drawing (not that that's such a bad thing), as he used simple, flat, bright shapes contained by rather crude black lines.

The colours he picked had never before been seen out together and, at the time, must have been a bit of a shock as one French clever-Dick (or Pierre) labelled his paintings 'barbaric harmonies'. Matisse was, no doubt, influenced by the oriental carpets and tapestries he loved so much. Their all-over patterns and hot North African colours can be easily recognized in just about everything he did.

Unlike Rousseau, Matisse's brilliance lay in what he left out of a composition as opposed to what he left in. Often his later pictures, like *Harmony in Red* cannot be read in black and white reproductions, as they use pure colour only to create the form.

Other Great Fauve Names to Drop

André Derain, Georges Rouault, Oskar Kokoschka, Emil Nolde.

CHAPTER 30

Back to the Future

Primevalism

CONSTANTIN BRANCUSI (1876–1957)

A Romanian sculptor who came to Paris in 1904, Brancusi liked what the old Fauves were doing but preferred to look closer at primitive stone carving. His famous sculpture, called *The Kiss*, is pretty sensual . . . if you're turned on by watching two rocks getting it together. But I think his work often rather insults the primitives whom he strove to imitate. Maybe that's why he's known as a Primevalist. Anyway, whatever 'ist' he was, he had a profound effect on the sculpture of his chum Modigliani and particularly English sculptors like Henry Moore.

AMEDEO MODIGLIANI (1884–1920)

It's a very strange fact that when researching this book I found that quite a lot of art histories left out poor Modigliani. Not 'poor' because he died of drug addiction at the peak of his career, but more because of the reaction of art experts who resented his enormous popularity amongst the sort of people that

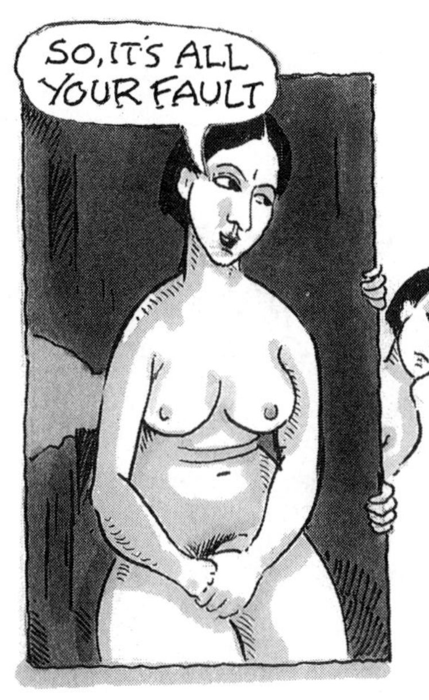

wouldn't have modern art in the house. The reason for this is fairly simple. If you look at the immensely successful paintings of 'high street' artists like Buffet (clowns crying), or Tretchikoff (green ladies), which sell by the cartload out of department stores and petrol stations, there is a similarity in their directness. Modigliani's portraits appear to be almost cartoon-like in their simplicity and have the same no-nonsense appeal as 'bad art'. Modigliani's paintings and later sculptures, however, have a peaceful and subtle beauty about them, much like primitive art, that is easy to miss on first glance.

HENRY MOORE (1898–1986)

If Picasso's Cubist women get the non-art-loving public hopping mad, then Henry Moore's sculptures are the 3D equivalent. His huge rock women, with as many holes as a Swiss cheese, have been a source of fun amongst the artistic illiterati since he started knocking them out in the thirties. Mind you, he said he wasn't trying to make a woman of stone, but a stone as sensuous as a woman. This apparently becomes obvious when one touches or caresses his work. I don't know, but I bet I could tell the difference in the back row at the cinema, sensuous or not.

Many art critics reckon he sold out in the later part of his life, producing work just to please the art establishment. He was certainly guilty of believing his own press, stating once that he was as great as Michelangelo (Michelangelo who? we ask ourselves).

Seriously though, whether or not one likes the work of Moore, he was to become the most famous English sculptor (and produced the most expensive holes in history).

BARBARA HEPWORTH (1903–1975)

Co-leader of the modern sculpture movement in Britain during the 30s, Barbara Hepworth was far less obvious and more subtle than Moore. She often worked in wood, using its natural form and grain to produce pieces with a finish and sensuality that often defied belief. The problem in modern galleries is that when you

succumb to the overwhelming urge to feel and fondle a Hepworth, you're likely to end up having your collar felt by some angry attendant.

Other Great Primevalist Names to Drop

Almost anybody whose name is associated with big lumps of rock with holes in, was influenced by these guys.

CHAPTER 31

No More Pretty Pictures

The Expressionists

My friend Paul, who I play darts with on Friday nights, reckons Matthias Grünewald, the sixteenth-century painter, was the father of Expressionism (mind you, he's a lousy darts player).

The movement started in the early twentieth century and reached its zenith during the First World War. Like Fauvism, it was a reaction against Impressionism and Naturalism, but although Fauvism is now regarded as part of the Expressionist movement, it was the German branch of the family that really carried the name.

If, like me, you're getting rather hacked off with all these stupid 'isms' and 'ists', then please bear with me. The only real use they have is for identifying and placing an artist in his or her time and culture span quickly. People always want to put each other in pigeon holes and artists and their followers are no exception. They usually started as snide nicknames, but like 'Punks', 'Hooray Henrys' or 'Yuppies' the insult actually stuck and in the end became common language.

I digress. The Expressionists were trying not to present the world as it hit the eye, but more what was going on in the artist's mind when he was looking at it. They wanted to show off their religious or social convictions in the roughest and simplest way possible, and with a bit of luck, while doing it really annoy the academicians. A most typical Expressionist painting would be *The Madwoman* painted in 1920 (the year tea bags were invented) by Chaïm Soutine. Although crude in its application, it tells us more about the subject than many more realistic paintings ever could. Earlier and more gentle Expressionists, like Van Gogh and Munch, led to a group in Dresden called Die Brücke (The Bridge) in 1905, who did really violent, aggressive work – and then the Blaue Reiter

(Blue Rider) group in 1911 who were still angry young men, but far more structured.

EDVARD MUNCH (1863–1944)

Munch was a Norwegian painter who hit the headlines when he made a lithograph in 1893 called *The Scream* which aimed to demonstrate how a sudden shock or excitement changes all of our sense impressions. Never before had an image caused such a fuss. Everything in the picture leads to the head and, in particular, the scream. Worst of all, we are left in the dark as to what the poor dear was so het up about. What really annoyed the general public, however, was that this and many of his other pictures were deliberately trying to be unbeautiful. It was all right for a caricaturist to mock and 'uglify' his subject, but 'proper' artists should really try to make everything look nice (hear, hear!).

Munch, and the Expressionists that followed him, felt so strongly about the crappy state the world was in, that to produce anything pretty or polished (like the academicians) was not only a total cop-out, but deliberately insincere, and really hypocritical.

It's almost funny. When Mr Hitler's National Socialists came to power in Germany in 1933, modern art was banned and all the artists exiled.

WASSILY KANDINSKY (1866–1944)

Kandinsky was a Russian and one of the Munich Blue Riders. He was the first to try to draw something not to look like anything in particular. If you disapprove of abstract or non-figurative art, don't blame me . . . blame him. He thought the time had come to do away with boring old subject matter and try to achieve what he wanted to express by just using shapes, tones and colour.

Kandinsky was a real head case (or should I say mystic) who hated science and progress and longed for something he called 'inwardness'. Don't ask me what this means. All I can really grasp is his statement that pure colours can have psychological effects. For instance bright red can affect us like a blast on the trumpet (don't be silly, Wassily!), or the simple opposition of the complementaries red and green 'expresses the terrible passions of humanity'. Staggering along this line of thought he then attempted 'colour music', or music without any sound (wacky or what?), just tones and shapes as in *Composition IV (Battle)*. This 'interesting' work was probably the first painting that we now call 'abstract art'. Kandinsky must be the last guy to claim the title of 'father of modern art'.

PAUL KLEE (1879–1940)

A friend of Kandinsky's, Klee was a Swiss painter deeply impressed by what the Cubists were getting up, sideways, behind and along to in Paris. He was also a fan of primitive art and the crude, but expressive, drawings of little kids. You might well wonder, with a mixture like that, what his stuff actually looked like.

His first notable drawing was called *Twittering Machine* and looked very much like the doodles you used to scribble or carve on your desk at school when bored out of your brains. Critics have called his style marvellously economical and precise. One is tempted to agree, but then any simple scribbles could be called that. One expert goes as far as to say that this drawing is a 'complex of ideas about present-day civilization' (and my name's Pope John III).

To be honest, his work is surprisingly pleasing and even fascinating to the eye, especially if you like spindly, off-the-wall, cartoon-style drawing. Trouble with Klee's stuff, however, is that most people, even half a century later, are still looking for the joke.

GEORGIA O'KEEFFE (1887–1986)

Somewhere between a Fauve and an Expressionist, this American painter, who sounds a bit like a country singer, has never been more popular than today. Her weird but sensuous part-plant, part-landscape, semi-abstract paintings show a really strong sense of design coupled with a lyrical sense of colour. I don't actually like them that much, but that's art for you!

Other Great Expressionist Names to Drop

Ernst Barlach (sculptor), Max Beckmann, José Clemente Orozco.

CHAPTER 32

Italy gets Modern

Futurism

Everyone suddenly wanted to be on the Cubist artwagon. Up until now Picasso and Braque had stuck to nudes, guitars, newspapers and fruit bowls etc. Other painters, however, saw it as a vehicle to represent symbols of modern times, especially architecture and engineering.

Time for a new 'ism'. Italian artists and sculptors adopted the name Futurism in 1909 and released a manifesto rejecting everything that had gone before, which is, let's face it, a bit like adults calling children unnecessary. They went on and on about how wonderful machines were, until it was those very machines, in the form of guns, tanks and planes, that killed most of the poor misguided so. . .ldiers in the First World War. I suppose it wasn't that surprising that this almost sexual love of machines came from Italy. After all, they'd hardly developed beyond the donkey and cart.

FILIPPO TOMMASO MARINETTI (1876–1944)

The inventor of, and inspiration behind, the movement was a part-time organ grinder, part-time Fascist and full-time nutcase. He believed himself to be the most modern man in Europe and hated anything to do with the past. He rejected everything that had gone before, from Bellini to Wagner, and became the very first really 'bad boy' of modern art. If you want somewhere to heap the blame for the daft artistic happenings that became so popular in the 1970s, lay it all on Marinetti. Talk about lost causes. Not content with condemning the past, he started having a go at everything else, including, would you believe, pasta! He stated that it was 'heavy, brutalizing and gross . . . it induces scepticism and pessimism. Spaghetti is no food for fighters!'

I must admit, the last thing I would think of doing after a huge plate of spag bol is pick a fight with someone, but I don't need a flipping 'ism' to tell me that.

The trouble all his followers had, however, was how to turn all these half-baked rantings into good old-fashioned paint. So what did they do? Did they invent a new style to go with the blossoming of technology? No way! They dived straight back into the past and rehashed Pointillism and Cubism, producing naff paintings like *Dynamism of a Dog on a Lead* by Giacomo Balla. This was thought to be ever so clever as they reckoned it out-did photography, which was becoming all the rage. The other big names in the Futurist movement were Joseph Stella, Fernand Léger and the woman leader of the Russian version, the Cubo-Futurists (No! it wasn't a Latin-American band), Liubov Popova.

Suprematism

Defined as an early-twentieth-century form of Geometric Abstraction, Suprematism attempted to represent the visual world without using any objects, so achieving 'pure art'.

In what has been called one of the greatest leaps of symbolic and spatial imagination in the history of all art, the movement's founder Kasemir Malevich invented the Black Quadrilateral which was (when you get right down to the nitty-gritty) a black rectangle painted on a white background (no kidding).

There now follow some of the things that have been said about this monumental statement:

1) a concentrated symbol having multilayers of meaning thereby providing the content missing in Cubo-Futurism (yawn);
2) the eclipse of the sun of Western painting and everything based upon it (yawn);
3) a triumph of the old, of the East over the West, man over nature, idea over matter (yawn);

4) a modern icon, superseding the Christian Trinity and symbolizing a 'supreme reality' (yawn);
5) an elegant simplicity that belies the intense effort required to synthesize a complex set of ideas and reduce them to a fundamental 'law' (yawn).

OK, but when all's said and done it's still just a black rectangle on a white background.

It might be the very best black rectangle that the world's ever seen. So much so that some people might really like it on their living-room wall; and, more to the point, if Mr Malevich managed to offload it on someone for a pile of dosh, then good for him, but save us the lectures pleeease!

I'll tell you what: here's my version, called Squarish Black, and a brief paragraph on what it means:

John Farman
Squarish Black 1994

'Here we see man's basic struggle with his own environment. A synthesis of all idiosyncratic art that has gone before, but sympathetically rejecting that very past in order to interact with a future that must essentially refuse to accept the present.'

Suprematism fell to bits when the individual artists tired of talking garbage and decided to tack on to other movements (to talk more garbage). I must admit I get a little cynical when a piece of visual work needs a long explanation to justify its existence. I'm sure if I turned up at the offices of a flash fashion magazine and offered myself as a male model, it would take more than my silver tongue to convince them.

Constructivism

The particular movement they mostly favoured went by the name of Constructivism, which had been started by a Russian sculptor called Vladimir (aren't they all) Tatlin. The Constructivists wanted to use modern materials like Perspex, sheet steel, metal tubing and wire to create modern art. They made huge spindly constructions out of these things but, strangely, became more obsessed with the voids (spaces) they created than the constructions themselves. When they reached the end of this particular blind alley they decided to go one further and worship something called Productism. This daft movement decided there was no difference between artistic creativity and the sort of manufactured stuff you buy in the shops. After a while they realized that they'd finally hit a brick wall and had intellectualized themselves out of a job. Slightly crestfallen, the silly-billies left Russia to go West and join the double-Dutch De Stijl (The Style) group.

CHAPTER 33

Art Stinks!

Dada (1916–1923)

Everyone needs a bit of light relief during a war and the international 'anti-art' movement, Dada, provided just this, though the 'artists' concerned would have been the last to see it that way. They set out to ridicule art with a huge A (a sentiment that I commend deeply). They printed daft poetry made up of random words, set in random typefaces which made them look – surprise, surprise – a total mess. They used household objects to make their obscure sculptural statements, as in Marcel Duchamp's *Fountain*, a simple urinal with the name R. Mutt inscribed on it. Dada was another 'ism', set up to challenge all the values of existing art, such as the cult of beauty, which seemed to them so bally stupid and hypocritical at a time when Europe seemed hell bent on pulling itself apart and destroying all its young men.

Unfortunately, all satirical, breakaway, 'bad-boy' movements eventually yearn to be taken seriously, make money, and then, even worse, be respected. Dada was no exception and, almost as a symbol of this, was included in the Paris Salon des Indépendants in 1920. They therefore shot themselves well in the foot, preaching anti-art with the same holier-than-thou language as the people they'd set out to ridicule (*see* p. 146, the Black Quadrilateral).

Anti-art will always lurk like a dormant virus in the minds of many art students. Firstly it is a brilliant cop-out from having to master all the skills needed to be a professional artist, and secondly it is a reaction to the almost impenetrable élitism of the fine-art racket.

The first time it re-erupted was in the late 1960s and 70s when it strangely manifested itself not only in the visual arts as Pop Art, but in music as well. The punk-rock movement came directly out of art schools in and around London.

Marcel Duchamp and his merry men certainly have a lot to answer for. They practically invented all the conceptual art that was to come later. In fairness to him, however, he did actually make up the joke. If only he'd realized that we'd all have to listen to that same joke, in various increasingly ridiculous versions, for years to come.

MAX ERNST (1891–1976)

Not all the work that came out of the Dada movement was silly (although they might well have liked it to have been). Indeed some of it was fascinating and a breath of fresh air. Max Ernst, for instance, took literally the 'art is rubbish' claim and started grabbing old tickets, newspapers, food packaging, pressed flowers, rubbings from old bits of wood, anything he could get his hands on, and stuck them on the canvas, so producing . . . art – dammit!

Sounds pretty easy, eh! Not necessarily. It was the way that Max arranged them that made them fascinating to the eye. I suppose that seeing the beauty in ordinary household ephemera and elevating it to art, could be said to pre-date Pop Art, which wasn't to be seen for some fifty years. Many regard Max as a prime mover also in the Surrealist movement, but he was so brilliant and innovative that it's daft to even try to pigeonhole him in one narrow movement or another. His work grew and switched directions throughout his life.

ALEXANDER CALDER (1898–1976)

Alexander Calder, an American engineer, was the first sculptor to make a sculpture that moved on its own. He was heavily influenced by the Spanish painter Joan Miró (a guy), who did funny doodle-like images with the loops coloured in.

Calder took these shapes and made finely balanced, deliciously delicate constructions that could fill a huge room or sit on a tabletop. At first they were motorized but he soon realized that they would be far more interesting (and cheaper) if he took the criticalness of the balance even further so that the whole construction could move with the slightest draught or breeze, much like the leaves on a tree. Whether or not you like the kind of mobiles that hang in kids' bedrooms, with anything from Mickey Mouse to My Poisonous Little Pony hanging from them, they all derive from the work of Calder. Shame he never got royalties.

GIORGIO DE CHIRICO (1888–1978)

Just before the First World War, a strange young Italian painter went to Paris and met Picasso and Apollinaire (the poet). He signed up as a Dadaist, but luckily that's about as far as it went. When war broke out he went home having invented a totally new type of romantic landscape. It had a semi-magical, semi-sinister quality, that reminds the viewer of dreams that he can't quite remember. Endless deserted streets, long intimidating shadows, weird perspectives; unrelated objects set on a stage waiting for some weird drama to happen. Although he's still reckoned to be a Dadaist, de Chirico was, in my humble opinion, the first of the soon-to-be-opening Surrealist school.

Many artists before and since de Chirico have tried to create pictures that give the viewer this out-of-frame experience but few have ever succeeded. What I find refreshing about de Chirico's relationship with his work was proved by his answer when questioned about its deep intellectual significance. He said words to the effect of: 'Don't ask me, guv, I just do 'em!'

CHAPTER 34

In Search of Reality

Surrealism

The taking of objects out of context so they represent something completely different – the Dadaists' favourite trick – led fairly directly to Surrealism. The name was coined to express the yearning of young artists to achieve something more real than reality itself. This, they reckoned, is what the primitives and even children had been doing for years. But we all know that you can't go back to being a savage or a child at will, unless, as Freud said, it's in your dreams.

Surrealism started properly when a poet called André Breton published his *Manifesto of Surrealism* in 1924, which defined it as 'pure psychic automatism, by which it is intended to express . . . the true process of thought . . . free from external reason and from any aesthetic and moral reason' . . which freely translated means 'anything goes'!

Surrealist theory is saturated with freshly nicked concepts from psychoanalysis and, maybe, should not be taken too seriously. The idea that a dream can be poured out directly on to canvas is all right in theory, but seldom works in practice.

SALVADOR DALÍ (1904–1989)

By far the most talked about of the Surrealists and probably one of the most famous (or infamous) artists of all time. Nobody can ever be sure whether this weird man with the stupid curly moustache was a remarkable genius, a stark-staring, certifiably bonkers ego-maniac, or a tedious, attention-seeking, pretend eccentric. Whichever (if not all) is true, it can't be denied that Dalí produced the first modern art to appeal to everyone from the road sweeper to

the aristocracy (it still does); a kind of Paul McCartney of the art world (sorry, Salvador).

The reason for this is dead simple. Although images of floppy clocks, arms growing out of trees, dogs made out of fruit bowls, all set in weird classical landscapes, would normally have the man (sorry! person) in the street scratching his head, Dalí painted with such detail and dexterity that he could simply accept it. Many people who would describe modern art as pretentious crap will make an exception for Dalí. The moral of the story (and Dalí) is: you can get away with anything, if you present it well enough!

RENÉ MAGRITTE (1898–1967)

René Magritte, one of the most famous Belgians in the history of Belgium (name three others), came along later than Dalí, but though not quite as famous, his influence has probably been even greater. Although very much a Surrealist, heavily influenced by Ernst and de Chirico, his paintings are simply wonderfully executed visual jokes.

B
BACK SOON

Think about bizarre situations, be it a train steaming out of a fireplace, a man looking at the back of his head in a mirror, a pair of boots with human toes – Magritte churned out hundreds of these confusing eye-to-brain images.

He was, in my opinion, really a cartoonist. OK, a brilliant cartoonist, showing the way for others like Folon, Steinberg or the fab Gary Larson, but the fact that he painted his images in a scrupulously observed academic style, put them in frames and hung them on walls, elevated these jokes to fine-art status. Again, the man in the street, who tends to admire anything he can't do (and loves any joke he gets), found Mr Magritte just his cup of tea – like Dalí. I can't be certain what the woman in the street thought but I imagine she was pretty keen too.

His greatest influence, strangely enough, has not been in the world of art, however, but in the much more lucrative field of advertising. A huge percentage of posters, television commercials, magazine ads or pop promos etc. uses exactly the same point of reference. That is, find an everyday situation that everyone understands then introduce some huge incongruity. For example, take that recent series of beer commercials, in which the foreground characters are shot in the normal way, but the background action is filmed in reverse. The final result is a situation that first looks perfectly normal, but on closer consideration doesn't quite add up. Have a look next time you see adverts and see just how many use Surrealism. You will be amazed; it's all pure Magritte.

If it sounds like I'm belittling Magritte because of this influence on a basically hard-nosed, unscrupulous business, I'm not. Magritte was one of the first to show us that we take everything we see in front of us for granted. By switching things round and changing what we 'know' are basic laws of nature, he makes us realize that reality or truth is only based on what we have seen so far. Apart from which, as I've said before, although we see the same sort of visual juxtapositions every day in the media, it was René Magritte who made the joke up first.

ALBERTO GIACOMETTI (1901–1966)

Although busy working at the same time as Moore, Giacometti was closely linked to the Surrealists. He started what was probably one of the most fascinating and innovative periods of sculpture. His early work involved taking the natural shapes of large stones and seeing how little he needed to do to them to make them resemble something figurative, a bit like converting a doodle. For me the results are far more interesting than Moore's more contrived holey figures.

Giacometti then went on to make thought-provoking, often slightly scary Surrealist constructions out of metal, wood and anything else he could get his hands on. But it was his famous eerie, spindly metal figures, reminiscent of tribal totems, that really caught the imagination of sculpture lovers and made him one of the all-time greats.

CHAPTER 35

But Is It Art?

Neo-plasticism

PIET MONDRIAN (1872–1944)

Founder member of the 'I Bet I Could Do That' school of painting, Piet came to Paris in 1912. He was nine years older than Picasso, and claimed to be an Expressionist influenced by Van Gogh and the Fauves. I don't know exactly what it was, but something rather odd must have happened to him. He invented his own personal 'ism' called Neo-plasticism which hid under the aforementioned Dutch umbrella known as De Stijl (The Style).

The works which got him famous, when you get right down to it, consisted of a few horizontal lines (which he called female) and a few vertical lines (which he called male) with a few bright colours filling in some of the squares created.

Whole libraries of books have been written about how he, and why he, came to place the lines and how and why he chose which squares to put which colours in. Also it has been said that:

1) he wanted no distracting elements or fictitious associations;
2) his goal was pure reality;
3) he strove to achieve equilibrium through the balance of unequal but equivalent oppositions;
4) he arrived at his compositions by feel and because of an exquisite sense of geometric balance, so much so that forgery was, and always would be, impossible.

Maybe so, but I have just a sneaking feeling that given a bit of canvas, a few primary colours, a set square and some masking tape, I could have a few fair copies out by lunchtime.

Again, if you like this kind of thing then it's the kind of thing you like, but if someone tries to make you see something that you just cannot fathom, then remember your opinion is every bit as good as theirs – and you can quote me!

CHAPTER 36

Passionate Painting

Abstract Expressionism

Action Painting

Abstract Expressionism grew out of Surrealism just after the Second World War. There were two basic groups: the action painters and the colour-field painters. The action painters were a group of artists who didn't want the paint to represent anything in particular, but became obsessed with the paint itself. This broke away from Kandinsky, the first abstract artist, who admittedly didn't paint anything you'd ever seen before, but at least tried to make it look like something (eh?). Action painters preferred to let the paint do the work, and then asked the audience to make up their own minds about what they wanted it to be.

Abstract Expressionists got together, so they claimed, in reaction to the fear brought on by the nuclear age, and the subsequent cold war. A quote from a learned tome describes the movement thus: 'Action painters saw painting as a counterpart to life itself; an ongoing process in which the artist faces comparable risks and overcomes the dilemmas confronting him through a series of conscious and unconscious decisions in response to both inner and external demands.'

Personally, I'd find it just as easy to believe that they were reacting against the price of frozen peas (which probably weren't invented yet).

JACKSON POLLOCK (1912–56)

Jackson was by far the most famous of the action painters. He'd been rather a good (whatever that means) Expressionist and then Surrealist, but obviously woke up one morning with a scheme to get rid of all the half-used tins of paint hanging around in his studio, get home very early after work and make more cash than he'd ever made before.

Do you remember the fuss when Ruskin got sued for accusing Whistler of 'flinging a pot of paint at the public's face'? Well, Pollock went for it in a much bigger way and totally smothered the public's face.

He would lay the huge, unstretched canvases on the floor and fling, pour and dribble layers of paint and then play with it, using anything he could get his hands on (as long as it wasn't a boring old brush), until he'd got the effect he wanted. Whether one likes his paintings or not, one is forced to admit that the finished products are almost magnificent in their audacity, power and pure energy. Actually, who cares how the paint got on the canvas? The brush is simply a rather hairy convention passed down through history and, anyway, nobody seemed to mind when artists in the

70s started using spray guns (unless it was on bus shelters). The real objection to Pollock's unconventional method was the old 'I could have done that' argument.

This old chestnut could, of course, be levelled at nearly all famous modern artists. Anyway, the reply is simple:

Sure you could have done it . . . but you didn't!

Other critics have since written about the deeply significant meanings of his work, but the artist himself would have thought this all a load of 'Pollocks'. He insisted that painting for him wasn't an intellectual exercise, claiming he had no recollection of what he'd been doing while flinging paint around, and that he was guided by 'the forces of nature'. So much so that when the trance was over, he had to 'get acquainted' with the finished canvas (and if you believe that, you'll . . .).

Unfortunately, he could well have been in this condition when a car crash cut short his career in 1956.

Back to Brushes

Other action painters refused to part with the brush, although it's fair to say that much of the work by de Kooning, Dubuffet and Krasner looks as if the brush could conceivably have been in the grasp of something not quite human. In fact, I remember when I was a kid the pop-anthropologist (and master of the blinking obvious), Desmond Morris, had a pet chimp called Congo on telly who had several extremely successful (if you're into bananas) exhibitions of his Expressionist work. . . My case rests!

Dubuffet's *Corps de Dame* gives one a fair idea of what they were up to. The unfortunate, somewhat flattened Dame looks as if she'd been in the car with poor Pollock. When confronted with a statement that the painting looks as if any child (or chimp) could have done it, Dubuffet came back with the following:

> The female body has long been associated with a very specious notion of beauty . . . which I find miserable and depressing [funny lad!]. Surely I am for beauty, but not that one . . . I intend to sweep away everything we have been taught to consider – without question – as grace and beauty and to substitute another and vaster beauty, touching all objects and beings, not excluding the most despised . . . I would like people to look at my work as an enterprise for the rehabilitation of scorned values, and . . . a work of ardent celebration.

All very well, Mr Dubuffet, but if that Dame's your idea of beauty, I'd hate to have met your missus.

Colour-field Painting

The second group of Abstract Expressionists were called the Colour-field Painters and got together because they didn't like the way action painting was going. They preferred to paint all the canvas in thin colour-washes, claiming rather smugly to have solved the conflicts expressed by action painting.

After the mid-fifties action painting was all washed up, probably because the artists couldn't bear the state their shoes were getting into.

MARK ROTHKO (1903–1970)

The most prominent of the Colour-field movement was Mark Rothko, soon to be king of the 'What's it Meant to Be?' school of painting. He knocked out huge, one-coloured canvases inside which were usually a couple of thinly painted, different-coloured rectangles. If you have a nasty damp patch on your wall don't buy a Rothko to cover it, as it'll look much the same (and cost a fortune). This is a crude and uneducated accusation, of course; I'm sure all those people who stand for ages (albeit nervously) in front of his work in galleries must see the deeper meaning. After all, critics have claimed that in less than a decade Rothko subdued the aggressiveness of the action painters so completely that his pictures breathe the purest contemplative stillness. This of course could be true . . . but what if there's nothing in them *to* think about?

As far as some people are concerned, however, Rothko was either a darn good salesman, or those shapes and colours have a deeper meaning that passes right over my head. I couldn't, however, say that Rothko's work does nothing for me at all. When I sat recently for a few minutes in the Rothko room at the Tate Gallery a strange feeling came over me: I started to become deeply depressed. I then went straight down to the bar and cheered myself up. Having said that, it appeared that poor Rothko found painting depressing as well, for his work got darker and darker as the years went on until, finally . . . he topped himself.

HELEN FRANKENTHALER (b. 1928)

Some artists managed a cross between the action painting of Pollock and the more subdued colour-field stuff of Rothko. One of these was Helen Frankenthaler, who produced beautiful paintings in which she used the oil paint as a delicate stain, almost like a watercolour. Her painting called *Rapunzel* (1974) is a masterpiece in basic design (even if you can't see head nor tail, let alone hair, of the subject).

Other Colour-field Painters' Names to Drop

Morris Louis, William T. Williams, Barnet Newman, Clyfford Still.

CHAPTER 37

Art Goes Hard

Hard-edged Painting

Artists in the mid-fifties became bored not only with Abstract Expressionism but particularly with Rothko's soft-edged rectangles. They looked longingly back to Mondrian and started to produce very graphic paintings where the colours met on a hard edge. Ellsworth Kelly's imaginatively titled *Red, Blue and Green* reminds me of the dreadful colours that fashion designers used for girls' frocks in the silly 70s.

Frank Stella used metallic powder mixed in hi-polymer emulsion to produce *The Empress of India,* a series of immaculate stripy orange chevrons stuck together on a black background (rather like shiny, modern wrapping paper). Hard-edged painters were determined to make their work look as far from hand-made as possible, though the reason is somewhat obscure. Stella gets my 'Man of the Match' award by silencing all the pompous writers about art when he made this monumental statement: 'My painting is based on the fact that only what can be seen there is there... All I want anyone to get out of my paintings ... is the fact that you can see the whole idea without any confusion.'

I wish someone had told the Abstract Expressionists that!

Op Art Painting

Other painters were exploring the physical and psychological process of vision. The trouble was it never really caught on, probably because the paintings always looked as if they'd be more at home in a science lab than an art gallery. Indeed, if you had them in your front room, they'd shortly send you blind or mad, as these abstract images become almost hypnotic if you look at them for more than a few seconds. Perhaps the most important exponent of this, dare I say, rather superficial art movement was Victor Vasarely, a Hungarian living in France, while Britain had Bridget Riley who had her fifteen minutes of fame (an expression coined by Andy Warhol) in the mid 60s.

Strangely enough, Op Art had a far greater influence on the fashion industry than anything else. French designer Courrèges used black and white checks and stripes on many of his shiny PVC outfits. Since then even Mondrian's images have been used by fashion designers stuck for an idea of their own.

Pop Art

Many great art historians and critics would have it that Pop Art was also superficial and a mere blip in the history of art. This could well be because the imagery used was essentially low-brow and always popular. It's funny, 'experts' or enthusiasts hate to see their pet subject popularized and brought in front of a much larger audience, like televising a favourite book. It's their baby, and they don't want the mystique shattered.

The origins of Pop Art are a bit obscure. Americans like to claim it as their own, because much of the imagery was US inspired, and with a few exceptions, the greatest exponents of the art came from across the pond. Most historians claim, however, that it began in London in the mid 50s when it was referred to by critic Lawrence Alloway. The Americans were right, however, as the real inventor of Pop Art was an American called Stuart Davis who, as early as 1924 – and way ahead of his time – was painting household objects and advertising ephemera in a brilliant hard-edged manner.

One must also be fair to Dada and particularly Duchamp who was really the first to point out that 'the thing itself' could (and should) be taken as seriously as a nice painting of it.

Pop Art came at this another way. Pop Artists would take a common, everyday, taken-for-granted, hardly-ever-looked-at object and paint a loving portrait of it. Let's face it, if you grab something dead ordinary like an ice lolly, for instance, and blow up a photo of it to twenty feet, then paint it absolutely straight on to a massive canvas, it's going to command a presence and power that even *it* never dreamed of. Maybe Duchamp was right in thinking that, in artistic terms, his 'urinal' was as important and beautiful as the statue of the Venus de Milo (and far more use). It's all a question of hype.

Pop Art came directly after Abstract Expressionism and showed two fingers to all the pomposity and excesses of artists who found it necessary to justify their often obscure work with words. Dada had been similar but had, unfortunately, simply replaced one set of boring words with another.

The movement first came to the general public's notice in a big way when Richard Hamilton produced one picture – in one exhibition. It was titled *What is it that makes today's homes so different, so appealing?* and was a wacky collage of a modern middle-class living room full of household objects with a muscle man flexing his biceps to a bimboid blonde sitting on the sofa.

There followed a refreshing period in art. Never had painting and sculpture run so closely with what was going on outside. In Britain painters like Peter Blake, Allen Jones, Peter Philips and later David Hockney were, at last, just ordinary guys who did what the rest of us did, and painted about it. It really put the art establishment's nose out of joint, until they realized that there was a huge amount of cash to be made. Pop was then, surprise, surprise, elevated to art with a capital A.

In the States Pop Artists were having a ball. The wacky New Yorker Andy Warhol scandalized the art world by not only producing a vast canvas of a Campbell's soup can, but also by freely exhibiting his wild bisexual lifestyle for all to see (and enjoy). It was he to whom I referred earlier as having made the statement that 'In the future, everyone will be famous for fifteen minutes.' He was . . . and for an awful lot longer.

Claus Oldenburg was busy making ginormous soft, blow-up

hamburgers and telephones out of canvas and plastic while Roy Lichtenstein busied himself enlarging newspaper comic strips to the point where they almost became abstract shapes. Other painters like Jim Dine, Robert Indiana and the great Larry Rivers reached almost pop-star status among young people fed up with being told that they should be able to understand Abstract Expressionism.

OK, maybe Pop wasn't a deeply meaningful art movement; but for many it was like releasing a long-suppressed fart. The Emperor could at last go out without his clothes and not give a hoot who saw him.

DAVID HOCKNEY (b. 1937)

Of all the painters of the British Pop Art movement, Hockney was the one to endure when, like yesterday's Mother's Pride, Pop passed its sell-by date. I think that our David would have been a fine painter in whatever age he lived. Almost like an enduring rock or film star, Hockney ducks, dives, parries and interprets all the fashions as they come and go, leaving a trail of imitators in his wake. Like Pop Art (and pop music), everyone understands a Hockney. His homosexuality is obvious and on display, and his love for the semi-sleazy, always sunny, life of California pours from the canvas. Over and above this, it is his fine sense of composition and draughtsmanship that link him with all the figurative masters of the past. Even his latest Polaroid collages add a fresh new dimension to a Cubism forgotten for half a century.

Photorealism

If you can see the point in photorealism then please let me know. Known also as Hyperrealism and Superrealism, it lived for a short period during the 70s in America. Artists like Malcolm Morley, Richard Estes and Chuck Close would take amateur snapshots, blow them up to painting size and then copy them to the last blemish. The nearer they got to the real thing, the better it was judged to be. For me it's a bit like making a cathedral out of matchsticks. A whole lot of painstaking and skilful effort just for the sake of it being a whole lot of painstaking and skilful effort. One painter who did seem to take it a bit further was a young American called Don Eddy. He managed to copy photographs, tightening up all that was out of focus, and flattening all the tones so that the finished work had an almost hard-edged, non-figurative and at times almost – yes – Abstract Expressionist feel.

CHAPTER 38

The Last Straw

Performance Art

Of all the 'art' forms that ever were, Performance Art is the one most guaranteed to make the public's blood boil and the artist fear for his life. Again, that old terror Marcel Duchamp (king of non-art) lurks behind it all. Performance artists believed that since all works of art are by-products of a thought process, the actual thing that you hang up can be dispensed with altogether, along with galleries and even the artist's public. Intriguing or what?

The creative process, they thought, could be presented in any way you like, anywhere you like, and to anyone you like, as long as nothing touchable, seeable or permanent remains after the act of creation (sounds like a condom ad!). This anti-art stuff is pure Dada and comes perilously close to being simply theatre. The problem I have is that it appears to me like describing a sumptuous meal to someone who is starving, and then telling him that the description was quite sufficient.

Along with the Mamas and the Papas, Peace and Love, Flower Power and Timothy Leary, Performance Art was to become a charming, if somewhat daft, icon of the 60s. The performances were called experiments in perception and weren't exactly a theatrical production, nor an art exhibit, but more of an unexpected event, usually in an unexpected place like a parking lot, a factory or even a public loo. They'd use materials that would never have been associated with art, like rubber tyres, fat, ice cubes, dead budgies – you name it.

Again, like the Dadaists, the 'work' of the performance artists was supposed to challenge all aesthetic values, and throughout Europe during the 60s you could see daft people doing even dafter things to each other, all in the name of art. (Or do I mean non-art?) Fame? Confusion? I don't know. Does anyone out there know? Answers on a postcard.

In 1936 a woman stood all day in Trafalgar Square, London, with the whole of her head covered in flowers.

Wolf Vostell parked his car across a railway line in Germany, invited an audience, and waited for a steam train to come along and smash it to pieces. He called the 'performance' *Nien-9-de Collagen*. If he'd used a Volvo they could have all watched the train being destroyed instead.

Jim Dine, in 1960, produced *The Smiling Workman*, in which he drank from a can of paint and then flung himself through a canvas on which he'd scrawled 'I Love What I'm . . .'

Sculptor Piero Manzini had a brilliant idea for making a lot of easy lire in 1967 by simply writing his name on people. Each punter would receive a certificate of authenticity which read: 'This is to certify that x has been signed by my own hand and therefore, from this date, is to be considered an authentic and true work of art.'

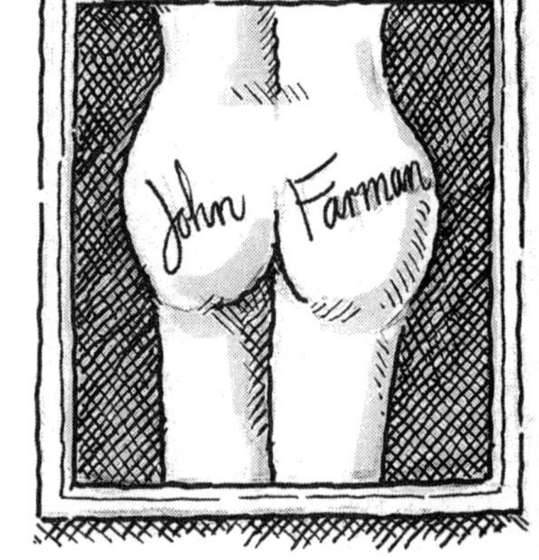

Anyone wanting to be signed by me, should send a self-addressed envelope containing a cheque for, say, two thousand pounds (extremely reasonable), and I should be only too happy to oblige.

Back in Germany in 1975, Ulrike Rosenbach spent much of her time wearing a skimpy white leotard, while shooting arrows into a statue of a fully dressed Madonna and Child. The performance was called *Don't Believe that I'm an Amazon*. (As if I would!)

Mind you, it wasn't the first time that the unhappy pair had been in that situation. Remember Raphael's *Nymph of Galatea* with all those fully armed cherubs and angels flittering round poor Mary's head? If you think all that a little odd, what about Victor

Trasov who, a year earlier, got off on walking the streets of Vancouver dressed as a peanut sporting a top hat.

During the Punk period in Britain a delightfully named Performance Art troupe Throbbing Gristle showed off their highly intellectual piece *Rectum in Outer Space* at, can you believe, the Architects' Association. One of the performers, Miss Cosy Fanni Tutti, also had a well-paid job as a model for porn mags. When this got out, our moral guardians, the tabloid press, and that model of respectability, Parliament, started a huge row in which the Arts Council, who had part sponsored the event, were accused of wasting the tax payer's money. Poor Throbbing Gristle were then banned from all non-private galleries throughout the Queendom.

Quite honestly, they sound a darn sight more entertaining than a pile of house bricks – yes, really! *see next page* – and at least they went home when they were finished.

My very favourite of all, however, is an English sort of sculptor who, thank the Lord, doesn't take himself (or art) seriously. Bruce McLean does pieces with enigmatic titles like *Waiter There's a Sculpture in my Soup* or *He Who Laughs First Makes the Best Sculpture.* My favourite McLean happening, however, was called *Crease Crisis,* which was a film made in homage to Victor (arguably Hollywood's worst actor) Mature's raincoat! He follows the tradition of that other great British loony, Bruce Lacey, who saw no reason why art with a middle-sized F shouldn't be mixed with entertainment with a huge W.

CHAPTER 39

Those Beautiful Bricks

Very Modern Art

The Minimalists . . . not many people had heard of Carl Andre in the early 70s, but by the end of 1978 he was probably the most famous (or infamous) 'artist' in Britain. It was he who created the sculpture called *Equivalent III* which was displayed, if that's the word, in the Tate Gallery, London. Never was the 'a child of three could have done that' or the 'call that art?' or the 'why doesn't that idiot go out and get a proper job?' brigade so vocal.

Andre's masterpiece consisted of 120 ordinary house bricks neatly laid out on the floor in a two-brick-thick rectangle. He was part of the Minimalist (or Get Home *Extremely* Early) movement and reckoned the bricks slotted into the formal debate about contexts. The paradox of such works, said Robert Hughes in his mighty book *The Shock of the New*, was that 'they staked everything on the institutional context for their effect, while claiming the density and singularity of things in the real world'. This, I think, means that while a pile of bricks looks a bit weird in a smart art gallery; on a building site it's quite at home (wow! ! !). This, of course, might seem fairly obvious to you or me, but the Tate Gallery parted with eight hundred of their very best quids to find this out.

Not for one minute do I blame Mr Andre, or any other of the Minimalist artists, come to that. Anyone who can turn up at one of the world's most famous art galleries and sell them something for loads more than he paid for it has the John Farman seal of approval. To be serious (for once), the Minimalists were fed up to the back teeth with the 'gestural' painting of the Abstract Expressionists who were so intent on making their pictures personal to them, like pictorial autographs. They preferred the Hard-edged painters like Frank Stella or Ellsworth Kelly, and even the work of the dubiously talented Barnett Newman in the early 50s. One of Barnett's most famous paintings was titled *Vir Heronicas Sublimis*, which was a largish red canvas with four, not that brilliantly painted, thin vertical lines.

Minimalist sculptors, much like the Constructivists, got really turned on by impersonal manufactured articles like steel tubes, sheet metal or the aforementioned bricks. Their excuse for the apparent simplicity and easy-to-do-ness of their art was (and is) that, although it might have minimal art content, it hides a complex intellectual message (an easy way out of anything, methinks!). Their work, they reckon, challenged each beholder to experience 'a layered and complex aesthetic response based on each individual's expectations and prejudices'.

This, as you might have realized, creates open season for anyone with a scrap yard who can write a load of pseudo-intellectual bull and persuade someone to believe it. Luckily you don't get that many scrap-yard owners who can actually write, otherwise they'd all be at it. Minimalist art seldom moves outside its own little closeted arty world, which is probably just as well, if you can remember what happened when Andre's brick sculpture escaped into the gutter press. Don't think I did miss all Minimalist art, however. Some of the works have an uncanny, overpowering effect on the observer, due almost totally to their monumental scale. Mathias Goeritz's huge steel structure called (cleverly) *Steel Structure*, made as early as 1952, or Ronald Bladen's *Cross* in 1967, were designed to be walked through and around and are good examples of this.

When you come across a Minimalist sculpture, in a park, or outside a modern building, just ask the questions: 'Does it look right here?' or 'Do I like it?' If it does and you do, then for you it's art and that's all you really need to know.

The very latest version of Minimalism, called Hyper-minimalism, takes the movement to its logical conclusion. Michael McMillan in his brilliantly titled *Untitled No. 42* now showing at the Liebervitz Gallery in New York simply delineates an area by a square cordon and leaves the rest to the viewer. Mr McMillan justifies his 'art' by the following statement: 'The human brain is capable of thoughts and images that exist without the need of definition by earthbound materials. I create a void in which thoughts and dreams may move freely, only bound by the dimension chosen. *Untitled No. 42* can be anything that occurs when my work is encountered.'

CHAPTER 40

Saving Studio Space

Land Art

In the 60s a group of artists reacting against 'the urban sophistication of Minimalism' (here we go again), decided that they didn't want to show their work in galleries or anywhere else for that matter, apart from where it was actually made. They would (and still do) scurry out from their smart studios in four-wheel-drives, often with nothing more than a shovel and a camera, to pitch up in the middle of nowhere and proceed to do wacky things with nature itself. Richard Long in England left little piles of stones everywhere, and wrote incomprehensible poems to them. In the States James Turrell decided to change the look of a volcano in Arizona and as far as anyone knows, is still digging. Robert Smithson took his bulldozer and built his crazy but wonderful *Spiral Jetty* on the edge of the Great Salt Lake in Utah which could only be viewed from hundreds of feet above and unfortunately sank when the lake decided to fill up.

Walter de Maria produced *Lightning Field* which consisted of four hundred needle-tipped stainless-steel poles covering one mile by one kilometre of New Mexico desert. It looked rather like some gigantic bed of nails and was designed to attract bolts of lightning from the many electrical storms (please don't ask why). De Maria's 'art', a bit like performance art, happened at the split second when the lightning hit one of the conductors. He later went on to produce two mile-long white lines in the Nevada desert and called it suprisingly *Mile Long Drawing*.

So, if you want to go into land art, all you need is a camera, an idea and a private piece of land where no one can either observe you or, worse, fetch a couple of burly nurses from the nearest psychiatric hospital.

CHAPTER 41

As the Paint Dries

Art in the Last Fifty Years

'Isms' and 'Ists' have largely disappeared over the last fifty years as artists no longer seem to need to group together as they did. This of course makes it more difficult to summarize what's been going on in terms of movements, so I think the best thing would be to mention a few random artists, as yet unmentioned, who have made some impact during this period. If I've left out your favourite – tough!

SIR STANLEY SPENCER (1891–1959)

Justifiably famous for assuming, at a cultural meeting with Chairman Mao in China, that the mighty leader would, of course, know he came from Cookham, Berkshire, Spencer was one of our best loved and most eccentric painters. Looking like something between a naughty schoolboy and a pervert, he painted funny, sad, and sometimes extremely explicit pictures; all in the same sometimes tortured, sometimes twisted, but always unique semi-realistic style.

L. S. LOWRY (1887–1976)

Much argued about member of the modern Primitive school, Lowry (a former rent collector) was 'found' late in life and hailed by some as a genius. I think this a little strong, though it cannot be denied that his paintings of northern urban scenes appealed to a wide public and made him a very rich old man.

Again, his work was easy for the common man to understand and although he wasn't actually very good at it (painting, that is), his streets, teeming with little matchstick-like people, certainly gave value for money.

Far from being a great painter, Lowry must give hope to all those ordinary people daubing away in their front rooms, dreaming one day of being discovered.

WALT DISNEY (1901–1966)

Not a painter, not a sculptor, not an architect, not even a fine artist with a big F or A, Walt Disney, despite being none of these things, introduced generation after generation of kids and non-visual grown-ups to a world of fantasy that they could all understand. He was probably in the same league as Leonardo, if one regards innovation and vision as the major qualities of the great artist.

Walt built a world that not even the company that has now replaced him can totally destroy, and doubts as to his place amongst the world's great artists should be dispelled by one viewing of either his 1940 creative masterpiece *Fantasia* or, arguably the finest animated movie ever made, *Pinocchio.*

Many might say that Disney didn't actually create the work with his own hands, relying on the talents of a bunch of almost unheard of 'assistants'. This might be true, but if that's the case, try naming any of Leonardo's, Rubens' or any of the other great masters' helpers. None of the Disney studio's great work could have existed without the master's direction (as can be seen from what's happened since).

FRANCIS BACON (1909–1992)

One of Britain's most famous modern figurative artists, Francis Bacon always denied being an Expressionist, claiming modestly that he hadn't anything to express. If you can imagine a butcher who decided to be an Expressionist painter, you'll get some idea of what the appropriately named Bacon is about. If you like paintings of people who look remarkably like legs of lamb or huge pork chops then he's your boy. As for me, despite his vast reputation, I find his work a little samey, and predictably ugly – and I'm not even a vegetarian! If I want meat I tend to go to Sainsbury's or look at the work of Chaïm Soutine, the Expressionist, who did the whole business back in the 20s.

Having said all that, Bacon's work has an undeniable presence and power that demands to be either loved or hated. Anything that provokes a reaction (within reason) has to be a good thing.

EDWARD HOPPER (1882–1967)

Many people, myself included, regard Hopper as really an illustrator, in the same vein as Norman Rockwell, the other great visual reporter of America. He did, in fact, study illustration in the States before learning to paint big pictures in Paris. God knows why he went there; he hated Bohemians and hardly spoke to anyone 'on the main art scene'.

When he got back in 1908, he illustrated for a while to make a few bucks before what was to become a lifetime of painting an America now largely lost. If you can imagine Impressionism with a slightly slick American accent then you have Hopper. If you can imagine a slightly ominous, almost de Chirico-like dream quality, then you also have Hopper. His use of light and shadow gives his work an atmosphere rarely equalled: a sense of loneliness that can send a shiver up your spine.

CHRISTO (b. 1935)

In 1920 the American Man Ray tied up a sewing machine in a blanket. Since then Conceptual Artists have become slightly obsessed with this rather silly idea. Christo must have put the tin lid on the art wrapping game, covering up bridges, cliffs, and even whole islands.

I will admit that his work, though totally potty, is quite sensational in its scale and audacity. Having said that, on seeing many examples of his work only two words spring to mind . . . *so what!*

In a world where over a fifth of the population lives below the poverty level, it seems fairly outrageous that some stupid bu . . . Bulgarian should be given huge amounts of cash to please a whole bunch of arty clever-dicks. Perhaps Mr Christo should wrap up the whole stupid planet (followed by himself). That would be an end to all this nonsense.

JASPER JOHNS (b. 1930)

Regarded as one of the big boys at the beginning of Pop Art, Jasper Johns painted stuff like targets, flags and maps. For me, however, his work has only a little to do with Pop Art, following much more closely the conceptual stuff of Duchamp or the paradox of the Minimalists. To call him a Pop Artist would be a bit of an insult as his work was far 'larger' and more innovative. But he did set the stage on which Pop Artists could perform and star, and few of the later artists like Peter Blake would dare deny how much they owe to him.

HOWARD HODGKIN (b. 1932)

Howard Hodgkin is one of those artists who some 'experts' label as figurative, but for the life of me I can't see how or why. They obviously see, from their descriptions of his work, lots of imagery that mere mortals, like me, don't. Of *Day Dreams,* for instance, one critic wrote: 'One sees the chromatic richness and texture of paint, hints of pillows and bedcovers, and a window opening out on to the night'.

I'm sure if the artist had called it *Night at the Zoo* the writer might equally have described a few nocturnal animals seen through the legs of a giraffe.

Another famous writer on art said: 'The special aura of his work is an intimacy that verges on voyeurism but suppresses anecdote.'

Hodgkin's paintings, to be serious, show slabs of the most brilliant colour, that leap from the canvas without, for some reason, ever appearing garish or crude. Unlike many other abstract painters, Hodgkin doesn't rely on size for impact, seldom working larger than three feet square. His paintings are simple, passionate, beautiful and strangely original. They need no further explanation.

LUCIAN FREUD (b. 1922)

If you want your portrait done, and you want to look fab, don't ask Lucian Freud. Relative of the great Sigmund and the rather un-great Clement, Freud has become almost *the* people-painter of the late twentieth century. He once said that he always tried to leave the face till last, so that he could show expression through the body. The head, he claimed, is just another limb. It might be just another limb to you, Lucian, but I bet you'd have trouble carrying on painting without it.

You can almost feel and smell Freud's people. Every quirk and imperfection, every bulge and scar. His faces, despite what he claims, have the same right-under-the-skin intensity of expression as Rembrandt at his best. If ever the line 'a picture is worth more than a thousand words' was justified, it would be to describe the work of Mr Freud.

GILBERT AND GEORGE (b. 1943 AND 1942)

Gilbert and George are two artists, living in England, who realized very early on in their careers that the media is the message. They would turn up at galleries, paint their heads gold and stand around frozen, like camp shop-dummies, claiming there was no separation between sculpture and life (or themselves and dummies). The art world of the 70s thought it all too, too wonderful and the two inseparable lads became a bit of a cult. Unfortunately, what they produced, or what you could actually take home with you, was often rather predictable, being more like the work of a graphic designer or illustrator.

The moral of the story? If you want to make it big in modern art these days, and don't mind making a bit of a prat of yourself, follow in the footsteps of Gilbert and George.

Some Other Great Recent Artists' Names to Drop

John Bratby: British kitchen sink painter. Seen one, you've seen 'em all.

Reg Butler: British sculptor. Wonderfully welded figures.

Otto Dix: German painter and illustrator. Master of 'ugly realism'.

Allan Jones: British painter and sculptor. Famous in the 60s for his fetishist women.

Ron Kilaj: American painter. Complex pop collages.

Robert Motherwell: American Abstract Expressionist.

Ben Nicholson: British artist. Famous for his white reliefs.

Sidney Noland: most famous Australian contemporary artist. Name another?

Eduardo Paolozzi: British painter and sculptor. Became famous for his pop collages in the 60s.

Carry Doons: American Op Artist turned Grunge Artist.

Robert Rauschenberg: American avant-garde artist. Tongue-in-cheek Abstract Expressionism/Pop Art.

Man Ray: American painter, photographer and film maker. Very surreal.

James Rosenquist: American Pop Artist. Three-dimensional 'paintings'.

Joe Tilson: British painter and sculptor. One of the 60s Pop 'brat-pack'.

CHAPTER 42

Onward and Upward (Or Downward?)

'Art' in the Eighties and Nineties

Carl Andre's pile of bricks now seems positively academic compared to the ever-growing gang of artists who seem to be hellbent on making themselves a laughing stock. Strangely enough, these 'Neo-Dada-Surreal-Post-Expressionists' or 'Aren't We Extremely Clever-ists' are flourishing under the title Conceptual Art, either because their perception of the human condition outstrips that of you or me, or, dare I suggest, because there always seems to be enough stupid people around with loads of cash and an almost childlike belief that if someone tells you something is art then, by golly, it must be.

It would be a bit unfair to blame poor Carl or the other Minimalists for the explosion of daft art. One might do better to go back to the 60s and a German called Joseph Beuys who became a major figure in the European art scene and the prophet of the Expressionist revival.

He made a sculpture called *The Pack,* which consisted of a Volkswagen bus pulling twenty sledges, each one carrying a roll of felt, some fat, and a flashlight. Apparently poor Joseph had never been the same since an incident in the war when he crashed his JU–87 on the Russian Front. The story goes that he was saved by a bunch of wandering Tartar tribesmen who stupidly (I think) were doing their wandering in the war zone. Joe was in poor condition when they found him so, rather curiously, they smothered him in yak fat and rolled him up in felt.

Joseph was obviously grateful to this felt, and felt that he should feature it in his work, never more than when he used it to wrap up a piano so that it resembled an elephant and then painted two red crosses on its bum.

I think he must have landed on his head when he crashed that plane, for he later went on to make something called *How to Explain Pictures to a Dead Hare* in which poor Joe smothered his head in honey, covered himself with gold leaf (I suppose it makes a change from felt), tied an iron plate to his right foot, and murmured incomprehensibly for hours on end to the dead hare cradled in his arms. Not much of a job, but I suppose someone had to do it.

Upside-down Art

Also around that time in Germany a young painter called Georg Baselitz from Berlin spent fifteen years painting everything upside down (not him, it!) 'in order to emphasize their abstract qualities, while preserving a coarse symbolism of insecurity'. Georg went on, by all accounts, to be immensely rich, so who's laughing now?

To give some credit, however, to the people who produce the more recent stuff that I'm about to describe, I suppose they would claim strong links with Surrealism. This of course might be true but, as I said earlier when going on about Pop Art, the easiest thing in the world is to take a familiar object and change either its context, its size or its texture. It's not as if this is a new idea. Back in 1936 Meret Oppenheim produced a cup and saucer out of fur, called *Object*. Probably, because it was created by a woman, it was labelled 'the most intense and abrupt image of lesbian sex in the history of art'. Either I'm stupid, or I must have the cleanest mind in art history.

If one takes the work of the American Jeff Koons, who produced, for example, a thirty-seven-foot-high puppy made of flowers, one realizes that the only credibility it has lies in the fact that someone has actually bothered to make it. If you were to see a drawing of it or even have it described like a joke – 'Here, have you heard the one about the thirty-seven-foot puppy made out of flowers?' – it would be about as funny as an evening with Jeremy Beadle.

What I'm trying to say is that we are being fed the same old Duchamp/Magritte joke over and over and over again, whether it be a rhino on a stick (by John Baldwyn – £3,500) or a painting of Daffy Duck saying, 'Now I ask the jury – does my client look like the kind of person who could harm an innocent bird?' (untitled – £395), or the series of photographs of Keith Arnatt (in the Tate) showing himself in various stages of being buried alive.

Anyone with half a brain could come up with equally ludicrous juxtapositions by just looking round at the objects nearest to us. I know! I think I'll go and cast my typewriter in jelly with a trout set in the middle and call it *Writing about Fish*.

Talking of casting things, Marc Quinn, a British 'artist', got a buzz out of reproducing his head in eight pints of his own blood and displaying it, refrigerated, in a smart London gallery. Wouldn't it have been far more use, I ask myself, if young Marc had poured himself into some poor road-crash victim? At least it would have done someone some good.

Gina Pane, the Italian body-artist, eats as much minced meat as she can get down and then throws up in front of a delighted audience. The work is called *Nourishment*.

Wim Delvoye's bathroom installation tastefully decorated with representations of his own faeces was described thus in the art magazine *Flash Art*: 'It presents excreta as a beautiful process, an almost idealistic gesture of common humanity.' I reckon this description is as much of a load of crap as that which it describes. Still, who am I to criticize? Clever Wim sold it for $22,500.

A fascination with one's own bodily functions is no new phenomenon. Many years ago the Italian 'artist' Manzoni actually canned what he produced and sold it. Let's face it, as some wit once said, 'Where there's muck there's brass!'

This junk simply feeds a media desperate for something to write about when the British Royal Family aren't making fools of themselves, John Major isn't apologizing for himself or Michael Jackson isn't doing something weird to his already weird body.

There now follow a few examples of the sort of art that you might want to put on a shopping list for your nearest and daftest:

1) A nice pet from an artist-cum-genetic engineer, who wears a uniform and is currently working on a brand new animal based on a chicken.
2) A white ping-pong ball balanced on a jet of air, called unpretentiously *I Want to Spend the Rest of My Life Everywhere, With Everyone, One to One, Always, For Ever, Now.*
3) A dead shark in a tank of formaldehyde.
4) A close-up (extremely) photograph of the artist (Jeff Koons again) making love to his wife, a famous Italian politician (and stripper).

I tell you what. If you can't draw, paint, differentiate between colours but want a job that makes loads of money and gets you admired by the trendiest people in the world – panic not. Join this new wave of conceptual artists and fool some of the people all of the time.

CHAPTER 43

Bad Art?

Or Not?

Is there such a thing? After all, you might be thinking, if you swallowed my earlier premise that, at the end of the day, anything goes (providing you like it) a label like 'Bad Art' becomes impossible.

Bad Art, in my terminology, is all the stuff that you buy in places like department stores, petrol stations, car-boot sales (unless you uncover an Old Master) or Sunday colour supplements. Get the picture?

Apart from names like Tretchikoff (green ladies) and Shepherd (charging jumbos), most of the paintings seen in the millions of front rooms throughout the country are by people we've never heard of. The only feature that seems to pull all their work together seems to be slickness. Again, that's why the 'common man' respects Salvador Dalí and hates Picasso. Even that professional Australian Rolf Harris is appreciated for his undeniable skill.

To put it another way: those who have assumed that they simply can't make any sort of intelligible mark on paper, are blown away by anyone who can. In fact we all seem to admire skills we have not learned, otherwise nobody would watch that stupid bit in the Bruce Forsyth show where contestants make total prats of themselves trying to replicate some inane skill that some boring 'expert' has been doing for every minute of their every working day, year after tedious year.

That's also why people will part with their hard-earned cash to obtain anything that looks better than they can do themselves. This, of course, makes it open season for anyone who wants to flog a plate decorated with soppy kittens or a picture of the Queen Mum when she was a kid, painted by internationally renowned artists (that no one's ever heard of); let alone porcelain sculptures of Dickensian figures or galloping horses.

I'm not saying that the 'artists' involved aren't terrific craftsmen – Tretchikoff's famous (sick-makingly sentimental) painting of a drop of water next to an orchid dying on some old church steps, showed a facility close to that of Correggio or Vermeer (on a good day). But is it art?

OK, you might say, so what's the big problem with all that stuff? After all, we could all easily hang up a reproduction of almost any of the greatest paintings in the history of art, but we choose not to. Anyway, if art is about communication, then it must mean that guys like Tretchikoff who made more cash than almost any artist living or dead, must have it sussed better than most.

I think the answer is simple. 'Bad Art' is *easy* – not to *do*, but to *understand*. It makes no demand beyond what you actually see. Like a McDonald's Happy Meal, which can be consumed in about twenty seconds flat without any need to consider texture, flavour or nutritional value, a 'Bad Art' painting will sit politely above your rough stone, 'country-style' fireplace without so much as a whimper.

It's all a bit weird. People who wouldn't even consider going into an art gallery, let alone watch a programme about painting on telly, seem to need to have pictures on their walls for fear of being

regarded as Philistines. It would be a bit like me putting rackets or bats on the wall, when the mere idea of tennis or cricket makes me yawn. Adults, as opposed to kids, for some inexplicable reason feel guilty and embarrassed about not appreciating art. God knows why; I certainly don't lose any sleep over not really understanding sport and I certainly don't grovel and fawn over the guy that fixes my car when it won't go.

I think those old Egyptians may have got it right. The chap who came to paint pictures on their walls was no more or less important than the bloke who grew their food or fixed their telly. Perhaps if we stop thinking that artists have some fab God-given gift then we might start seeing what their work is really all about.

So?

So What?

If you've struggled to the end of this book, you might, if you're lucky, have some idea of how the art we know (and sometimes love) came about, and what you personally like or dislike.

Despite all that I said in the last chapter, when you get right down to the nitty-gritty, there's only one guideline you need go by when making up your mind. If the image you're looking at either tells you something about the subject you didn't know before, or simply makes you feel good, then for you it's art, and don't let any clever-dick try to talk you out of it. If, on the other hand, you like some of the stuff I've taken the mickey out of, then bully for you, as far as you're concerned, you're right, I'm wrong and that couldn't be more OK by me (but I bet I'm right really!).

Similarly, if anyone tells you you're thick if you can't get your head round some obscure piece of abstract art (for instance) then tell them (politely) to go forth and multiply. After all, it's horses for courses. Everything we do involves personal choice and preferences.

Let's face it: we eat the food that suits our taste and makes us feel good; we listen to the music that reflects our moods; we wear the clothes that give the impression we want to give, so why on earth shouldn't we choose our art the same way?

Index

Figures in **bold** show pages with illustrations